LISTEN
WHILE
YOU CAN

SUNI NELSON

Fulton Books, Inc.
Meadville, PA

Published by Fulton Books 2021

Cover layout design © One of a Kind Covers

ISBN 978-1-63710-948-9 (paperback)
ISBN 978-1-63860-518-8 (hardcover)
ISBN 978-1-63710-949-6 (digital)

Printed in the United States of America

To my huge and amazing family, which,
of course, is my inspiration

To all the pretty horses that we have known
and loved over the years—may your healing
spirits be blessed for all eternity

CONTENTS

WRITER'S NOTE

Every parent has a story. I'm a parent. I have a story. My parents, OMG, did *they* have a story!

I'll bet yours do too. I encourage you, if you are able, to listen while you can.

PREFACE

When I announced to my family that I was writing this book, I got a mixed bag of reactions. They ranged from "Really?" to "Hmmmmmm."

My son asked me why. Honestly, I had not considered why. The real, deep, in-my-soul answer seemed too big, too hard to explain. All I really knew, and struggled with for the better part of twenty years, was that this book *had* to be written. Trust me, I asked why too. Why me, mostly. I approached many published authors over the years in hopes they could take my notes and do it for me. Inevitably, they all handed it back and said I needed to write it. There was indeed a very insistent voice inside my soul that would not take no for an answer. Would not take "I don't know how to write a book" for an answer. I am pretty sure I am ADHD—unorganized, terribly forgetful, and totally inept for such a task. It still would not take any of those faults for an answer. Luckily, I ran into Jeff LaFerney, who offered to help and coach the project. The most important thing he did was give me permission to write it with my own voice and from my perspective. Once I actually figured out where and how to start, it seemed to pour out freely. It was still unorganized and a bit like a roaring flood splattering to the high heavens, so putting it all in the right order to where other people might be able to make sense of it was quite a challenge. Honestly, I was very unsure that the right words even existed to describe accurately the people my parents were.

They were complicated, complicating, opinionated, lively, beautiful people that lived with their whole hearts and shared all they had with anyone in their path. Both were way too stubborn not to overcome obstacles that would have buckled most people under such pressure. It just didn't seem right that they could pass by without something of that left behind, something that could be handed down to their grandkids and great-grandkids and friends and acquaintances. And even if you are someone who did not get to know them in life, through this book, I hope you know, now, you are one of those acquaintances blessed by their strong, tenacious, and above all, loving spirits.

Technically, all the above is what I was thinking when my son asked that question, but articulating it in that moment seemed slightly insurmountable. So I gave him the short answer: I want to write a book that will get me on the *Ellen* show one day. That's the dream: to meet Ellen. So here goes.

INTRODUCTION

I love the days when I could drive down our beautiful country road with all its curves and hills, savoring the views around each corner, the vast farms, fields, and mountain ranges peeking out in the horizon. Cattle and horses graze, often looking up to see who the traveler is that's passing by. We, in our arrogance, may think they don't know who we are, but they know. At least, they know if we are a regular or a newcomer and, in some cases, even know our names.

I drove or rode on that road thousands of times. I could almost drive it in my sleep, I think. I remember whizzing down it in excitement, anticipating going to movies, the skating rink, or wherever else it led on any particular day. I also felt the length of it as it seemed endless, trying to get to the hospital, nervous and scared due to some traumatic event or other. Those times I didn't love it so much because it seemed to never end.

On that particular day, a beautiful summer evening, I drove with windows down and the cool mountain breeze blowing through my hair. I loved it. I closed my eyes briefly, reliving many good and bad memories while wondering if I actually could navigate the road without eyesight. The car bounced over a small pothole, shocking my eyes open again. With a smile, I breathed deeply, knowing Lantana Road had a special place in my heart. Little did I know that that particular trip would open my eyes in a completely different way.

Arriving at my old homeplace, I excitedly exited my vehicle. I grabbed the bags of snacks I had picked up at the dollar store on the way—you know, the things you have to have while watching a movie: popcorn, chips, salsa, and of course, a variety of Little Debbie cakes. Those were Daddy's favorites. Mom's fave would be the popcorn.

I heard voices laughing and chatting long before I entered. I recognized Tim's, third born in the family, with his Southern cowboy slang saying "Aaaaawe haaaalllleeee," "Oh hell" or "All hell" (remains unknown for sure), drawn out unseemly long, followed by a "Ya don't say." My sisters and mom were laughing. I was sorry I missed whatever tale was just told. We always had so much fun when we gathered at the house, as we called it. My siblings and I all had our own homes by then, of course, but the house we grew up in would always be *the* house.

We gathered there often. Whether it was to watch movies, ride horses, or play music and boogie down, we knew it was going to be a good day. Listening to music and dancing had always been a favorite pastime among us. I learned how to polka around the open kitchen / living room. Larry, the second born, was especially good at the jitterbug. Come to think of it, he was just a really good dancer. Fast-stepping with him was like riding a roller coaster. You hung on and tried not to fall off! Tim was not a slacker in that area either. He was smooth as silk, Mom had said. Momma loved to sing and play her guitar and even had a band off and on throughout the years. Yes, hanging out at home was always fun. Momma and Daddy were the very center of it. On this particular evening, we were watching *Titanic*.

After we settled down with our snacks of choice, we put the VCR tape in the recorder, and the movie began. My brother Tim, all 6'4" of him, lay stretched out on the floor with a pillow under his chin. He was that long, tall cowboy that every girl in our little town swooned over. My two sisters, Carolina and Connie, were on the couch, with Momma in her rocking chair and Daddy in his recliner. Unfortunately, Larry was not able to be there that day.

One would think that Momma and Daddy had planned out their childbearing in perfect fairness. They had six kids: three boys, Tony, Larry, and Tim; then three girls, Connie, Carolina, and me. The oldest, dark-skinned and black hair just like Daddy, except for the green eyes. The next, fair complexioned and red or light hair just like Momma. And yes, it went like that all the way to the last. That's me. Perfectly even. I sometimes wondered how they did that.

I took my spot between Connie and Carolina. I liked being in the middle—of *everything*. I had already seen the movie twice and expected to cry *again*. Just like everyone else, some part of me hoped maybe this time Rose would indeed hang on to poor Jack.

However, during the video, I noticed Daddy kept getting up and walking out. Then he would come back in, sit down, get up, and go back out. This was not normal behavior. He seemed restless, bothered. I decided to follow him and see if I could find out why.

"Daddy, don't you want to watch the movie? It really is pretty good," I said.

He turned to look at me, and I saw big tears running down his cheek. My breath caught in my chest. I had seen my dad cry twice in my whole life. The first was when his father passed away. I was very small. I remember a room filled with people. The low murmuring of voices. Then I saw him sitting on the edge of a coffee table, head in hands. Crying. My daddy, who was stronger than anyone I knew. I couldn't imagine the pain he must have been in to allow himself to give in to that emotion, which, in his perception, showed only weakness. I remember being frozen for only a moment and then running to him and hugging him and kissing his wet cheek.

The second time, I was eleven years old. I heard the phone ring and Momma's tearful, panicked voice shrieking, "Tony…accident…hospital…coma." Suddenly we were whizzing down Lantana Road again, fast, very fast, hugging curves around Laurel Creek. I remember feeling like a ball of cotton had been stuffed down my throat. Suddenly we were back *there* again. The place where the very walls reek of loss. You smelled it as soon as you entered. We were in Bilbrey's funeral home, planning the funeral of Mom and Dad's firstborn child. It was the one place where everyone cried, including my dad for the second time.

All those memories were rushing through my brain as I scrambled to figure out why he would be so upset. Then he looked at me with those big dark-brown eyes and said, "I can't watch that movie." He choked slightly, saying, "I was on a ship that did that once." He barely got the words out.

I immediately felt confused. I pointed slowly toward the living room TV and asked quietly, "A ship that did *that*?"

"Yes," he replied. "It was during the war. I was trying to get home from France. I was supposed to be back by Christmas for a two-week stay. We left from Le Havre and had been sailin' for about three days when the storms hit. All I can tell ya for sure was that when they found us, we were approximately fifty miles from the coast of Norway. We had been pushed way off course."

Hanging his head and slowly shaking it back and forth, he said, "Those storms were rough. I ain't never seen anything like it. One second it was completely black you couldn't see your hand in front of your face, and the next, lightning would strike and you could see waves so big it made our ship look like a small toy. I had never imagined anything like that before."

"Was it a small ship?" I asked.

"No, it was a right good size. Held about three thousand men. Had about double that on it, though," he replied. Keeping his head down, not wanting me to see the tears that welled, he choked again, clearing his throat, and explained, "It was an old French warship. Had already been through WWI and around for a good while prior to that. Probably should've been retired. At that time, the military was desperate for ships and used whatever they had, I reckon." He then raised his head, peering off into the distance. "To this day, I don't understand how we didn't sink. It was broken and splintered apart in several places."

I gasped as I envisioned such a scene. My stomach tightened, and I suddenly lost all interest in watching a movie. I had never heard him talk about the war and certainly had never heard anything about that story. "But you were rescued," I said with relief, not thinking about the losses, only that my father had survived. "At least someone got to you quickly."

"Not real quick, exactly," he said, another tear spotting his cheek. "We held on for twenty-two days, stuck out in the middle of the ocean."

"Twenty-two days!" I exclaimed.

He gave a slow nod, still looking off into the distance.

Well, after a shocked pause, my brain actually started working again. I realized I needed to hear more. I needed to know more about the things that were never spoken of. Things that would explain why my mother always said never sneak up and give Daddy a hug when he slept. I did that once and almost got knocked across the room. I recalled hearing him holler out in his sleep many nights. Yet when awake, he was always so unruffled and soft-spoken. I don't remember ever hearing him actually raise his voice, except in his sleep. For a man with six kids, that is saying a lot.

In our family, thanks to big brother Larry—you got it, light hair and fair skinned, and the honorary boss of us—we have to *make* our family Christmas gifts. He can be a little bossy. He says buying them would be cheating. So we had to start thinking about our presents early, and sometimes ideas were hard to come by. I realized I might have stepped into something very special, *if* Daddy was up for it.

I was not sure if the war was something he would be able or willing to talk about. However, if so, we could come to understand him in a much deeper way, perhaps even understand the sadness that lingered just below the surface of his sweet and gentle voice. There had been times we had gotten small glimpses of it *unsuspectedly*.

With that thought in mind, I laid my idea out on the line. "I know a way you can get your Christmas project done early this year, and I could too," I said, using one of my best selling techniques.

I saw a twinkle in his eyes and then that familiar sly grin. He straightened a bit and asked, "Now, how's that?"

I explained my plan. It was very simple. All he had to do was talk. I would put his precious words on paper and make a book out of them for the family, knowing in my heart what a priceless treasure it would be.

And so we began.

CHAPTER 1

Always Start with Home Base

I had mulled over the things Daddy had said about the shipwreck all week. It was hard to concentrate on work. I thought of scenes in *Titanic*, how freezing cold the water would have been. How could anyone survive something like that for twenty-two days, lost in the North Atlantic in December? What would make someone strong enough to beat those odds?

Then I thought of that word, *home*. It is a powerful word. I know that from personal experience. Could that have been what he held on to so tightly?

Visions of what he had to get back to? When I think of home, I feel a warmth of love, safety, and belonging. I have to admit, it has helped me through times of trouble.

I remember as a kid being bullied at school. I was scared to death and dreaded going every day. Our, meaning my mother's mainly (definitely not Daddy's), religion was different. That fact seemed to put a target on my forehead for teachers and students alike. The thing they did not understand was that we kept the Sabbath. We also kept the Old Testament holy days, which meant I had to miss school for religious reasons quite often in the fall and spring.

I seriously doubt the kids would have noticed or cared if the teachers had not been so eager to show complete disgust. When things got really scary, I would close my eyes and think, *Soon I will be home.* The very word warmed my soul. I knew I would be safe there, loved. It gave me the strength to hold my head back up and keep pushing through. Could that be what Daddy had held to so tightly? Everyone has a mental life raft. I really wanted to understand what his was.

Not that being bullied in elementary school in any way compares to fighting a war thousands of miles from home or hanging on to a sinking ship. But in the end, perhaps what gets us through any level of life's most terrifying moments is not all that different.

I turned right at the Cumberland Mountain Retreat entrance sign. Daddy had sold much of the land to developers that promised to make a resort out of it. They eventually went bankrupt, leaving us with a half-done resort and a few small lakes. Fortunately, we also had Cumberland County's first swinging bridge going across one of them, a spot where my friends and I would sit and talk and sing for hours.

I remember us singing "Heartbeat, It's a Love Beat" by Tony DiFranco, one of my teenage heart-throbs. When it came to the part of the song where you hear a heartbeat, we would throw rocks into the water for sound effects, more of a *plop, plop* than a *thump, thump*. I can't wipe the smile off my face.

I pulled up to our ranch-style home with a basement, a house Daddy and our family built in the early seventies. I was small then, but I do remember being on the roof, laying tiles with the rest of the family.

What I remember most is the sadness laying heavy in the air as we worked on it. Larry had been drafted and would be leaving for Vietnam. Momma and Daddy tried to talk him into moving to Canada. Daddy said we could all go. We could start over. We would do fine, I'd heard him say. I cannot imagine how he felt watching his son march off to war after his own experiences. I totally understood the desperation, the willingness to pick up and leave, come what may, to protect his child.

Larry would not hear of it, though. He was as stubborn as his father, determined, always, to do the right thing. He said his friends were all being drafted, and he felt it unfair for them to go and him not. Besides, he thought they might need him, and he wanted to be there for the boys who had nowhere else to go.

I pulled around the circular driveway and parked my SUV just under the big oak tree that had provided shade for many a horse as they stood patiently getting new shoes on their feet. Well, not always patiently.

When I walked in the door, I heard the familiar sounds of *Gunsmoke*. Daddy loved TV Land and all those old shows. Momma had something cooking, and it smelled amazing. My nose led me straight to the kitchen. "What ya got cookin'?" I asked her in a singsongy style in remembrance of one of her favorite Hank Williams tunes.

She replied that she had a beef roast, mashed potatoes, and some of her famous homemade rolls almost done. Now, Momma was a smart woman, but in that moment, she must've had a lapse in judgment. She asked, "Are you staying for dinner?"

Yes. Definitely *yes*.

I actually was not sure when Daddy would be ready to delve into our project, this dredging up a past that he had worked so hard to forget, obviously failing to do so. I worried he might just change his mind. I left it completely up to him as to when and how, or if, we would proceed.

After a really exciting episode of *Gunsmoke*, he made his way into the kitchen and sat on a stool beside me at the island. "So where do you want to start?" he asked.

I have to admit, I breathed a sigh of relief. "Why don't we start at the beginning?" I asked. I felt pretty sure his unrelenting desire to survive might have been due to what he had left behind. I wanted to know what kind of life he had prior to the war. To find out what made him so strong and tenacious and, in the end, return from so many horrific experiences and still be this calm, loving man. On the surface, he showed no signs of damage. I had heard of so many who were unable to escape the ghosts of war.

I started by asking, "What was it like…your childhood, I mean? I know you have twelve other siblings. I know you guys lived and worked your own farm. I'd like to hear about your life before you were called to duty."

He thought a minute and then said, "You know where our old homeplace is, in Vandever?"

I shook my head yes. I was familiar with it. They had moved away from the farm and lived closer into town by the time I was born. However, I had driven by it several times.

That grin of his was wide across his face as he recalled a particular day in his youth. "I always liked to play pranks on the younger ones," he admitted. "It kept things more fun." Still grinning slightly, he said, "I remember hearing Momma yell, 'What's goin' on up there?' Then, right away, she knew I was up to somethin', so she hollered, 'What are you doin', Marshall Tabor!'" He turned to face me. "Your grandma heard the girls threatening to do all sorts of harm to me."

We were both laughing as he described the scene. I had heard about some of his pranks a time or two at family reunions.

"Then I heard her yell again, closer this time," he said. "'Marshall Perry Tabor, what have you done now?' She was at the bottom of the steps looking up at me. I was at the top, holdin' a big ol' black snake, chasin' the girls with it. Momma just stopped and stood there with that look on her face. I was doubled over laughin' as they ran and screamed. 'Will you please get that thing outta here,' she said calmly, putting both hands on her hips, tryin' to look stern. Momma wasn't scared of nothin'. Toughest woman I'd ever seen. 'Okay, Momma, I'm sorry,' I said, still grinnin'."

I'm sure Grandma didn't buy "Sorry" for one minute, I thought to myself. From what I knew about her, she was a no-nonsense kind of woman who ran a tight ship.

"'Stop scarin' your sisters half to death,' she had said." He tilted his head sideways as he explained. "That's when I caught sight of her out the corner of my eye. She was tryin' to hide a grin." He looked up slyly. "Then she headed back to the kitchen."

He got a more serious look on his face and continued, "Your grandma had her hands full. Thirteen kids, and well, you might as well say fourteen. Your grandpa was not a lot of help once he came back from WWI. Shell shock, they called it. He got really sick and was in bad pain sometimes. There were days he just stayed in bed all day long. Then sometimes, even in the middle of the night, he would take off running out into the woods. We would find him up in a tree. He'd hallucinate, thinkin' someone was after him. I couldn't really understand why he wasn't able to just pull his self together."

He lowered his head, as if a bit ashamed of something when he said, "I didn't understand then what he had been though. All I saw was how hard it was on Momma, and I hate to admit there was times I did feel a bit hard agin' 'em for it." He took a breath of what sounded like regret before continuing, "I shouldn't have felt that. I wish I'd been more understandin'."

He paused a moment, taking a cleansing breath to wash a bit of unearned guilt away, and continued with his story. "He never was able to go back to work after his discharge from the Army. He was on disability. He got a lump sum, and that was what he bought the farm and the house with. I remember hearing people talk about the Depression. We hardly knew there was one. We grew our own food and lived off the farm. Everybody had their jobs to do and, most of the time, did them without incident. Well, mostly." He grinned again. "I was teaching Paul how to snipe hunt when Mom came out and gave me that look again."

He looked at me, knowing I was recalling him teaching me to snipe hunt. I, too, had stood out in the middle of the field holding open a paper bag, saying, "Heeerrreee, snipy snipy." After all, that's the way it was done, of course.

"Your uncle Paul was about eight years old at the time," he continued. "The way Mom looked at me this time, though, was not reprimandin' or stern. What I saw on her face right then was worry. I could tell her heart was breakin'. I knew exactly what was weighin' on her mind. Hershel and I were both gettin' older. We would be called soon to go off to war. We all knew it. I had heard Momma whispering prayers, first that the war would end before we got old enough. Then that we would be protected somehow. Hershel would go first. He was the oldest. I had already made up my mind: once he got called, I would do whatever I had to, to go in right behind him. I had heard of other fellers who'd lied about their ages and got in early. Me and Hershel had never been separated." His voiced cracked with a weight of love for his older brother.

He looked down again, trying to hide from the emotion as he explained, "I hated the thought of breakin' Momma's heart, but there was no way around it. I would just have to get back and do what I could to help Hershel get back too. I sorta made that promise to myself right then and there. I had to make sure she did not have to lose either one of us." He said it so sternly, as if he had complete control.

"We kept up with all the war news by listening to our little radio every night. Things had not been goin' so well. According to everything we kept hearin', Hitler was all but unstoppable. Every report was about how he had taken control of some other country. We all knew if he got what he wanted in Europe, we would most certainly be next. America had not wanted to get caught up in that war. We hadn't recuperated from the last one yet. At that point, we weren't the superpower we are today."

That took me by surprise. I guess I had thought America had always been the most powerful country in the world. It had never occurred to me that was not so.

"All the reports we were gettin' made it pretty clear we didn't have much choice whether we were ready for it or not," he continued. "Hershel would turn eighteen soon, and I could see what your grandma was thinkin' plain as day."

He was peering out the large window that overlooked the front lawn. Obviously, he was not seeing the grass and trees or the long gravel driveway that disappeared through trees long before it met Lantana Road. Nor did he see that beautiful snowball bush in full bloom. That is what *I* saw. I sat quietly, breathing lightly lest I disrupt his thoughts as he described in detail one particular day. A day that apparently had been etched in his brain, quite *perfectly.*

He began softly. "I watched your grandma standing out on the front porch, bowl in hand, stirrin' slowly, watching us with that look on her face. In one moment, she was just appreciatin' where we were and what we had right then, all sleepin' under the same roof, safe and sound. I knew she would be simultaneously askin' God to keep it so. I'd watch her do this ever so often."

He stopped to take a deep breath. "I remember thinkin' sometimes you just gotta take one thing at a time. Learn to be thankful and not get too caught up in stuff you ain't got no control over. Most things have a way of workin' themselves out."

I had heard him say this often. In fact, I remember being very upset about something. He listened intently as I excitedly described why my world was on the verge of ending. Then in his calm, cool manner, he said those exact words. I felt instantly relieved. Honestly, I am not sure if it was the words he said or how he said them. I cannot even remember what it was I was so upset about now. I figured if he was that calm about it, he had to be right. It would all work out okay. Apparently, it did.

He paused again, pulling from his memory *something* of significance. Then he continued, "I watched over my shoulder as she turned and went back in the house. I decided to follow her inside. As

I stepped in, I stopped for a second and stood quiet, listenin'. Just took in those everyday noises like the screen door slammin' followed by the familiar creak of the hardwood floors. I heard the little girls upstairs gigglin'."

I saw a hint of a slow smile. He tilted his head slightly, as if listening intently. "Then I heard Momma and Christine, Willene, and Mattie talkin' in the kitchen, the sounds of pots and bowls and clatter that cookin' makes, the smells wafting from the kitchen. Maybe it was the first time I had paid much attention to all the natural aromas and noises of home."

As if a moment of clarity dawned, Daddy said, "That's what you carry with you, the voices, the scents, and the familiar sounds. You hold on to them, and you can get through most things all right, God willin'."

We both seemed to be pondering that thought as we sat in silence. I recalled the old farmhouse where he and all his siblings grew up. I concentrated, bringing the vision clearly to my mind. It was, *is*, actually, a pretty typical two-story farmhouse of that era, small compared to today's standards. I always wondered how they all fit in it. Probably no more than 1,200 square feet downstairs, and the upstairs part would be a bit smaller.

Grandma's favorite part, from all I have been told, was the wide front porch that stretched all across the front of the house. Every evening, the family gathered there on the cool summer nights. Of course, Grandpa would do his Bible reading. He usually managed to do that even on his worst days. When Grandma met him, he didn't know how to read and had never been to school. He learned eagerly, she had said. I wondered, because he was unable to work, if this made him feel a more viable part of the family. Perhaps it filed a void of self-worth.

It seemed he felt it was the most important thing he could do for them. He had been through one of the most brutal wars in history and was raising a house full of kids during what would come to be known as the Great Depression. Even tucked away on a remote farm, he knew the world was lurking close enough to shatter their bubble most any moment. Grandpa wanted his children to know where to go when the world mistreated them as it most assuredly would.

Grandpa loved to preach and often did so in the small community Baptist church. It was a time when daily family meals were special. This would be followed by time on the porch or, on cold winter nights, by the fire in the living room. Families had not been hijacked by the wonders of televisions and electronics just yet.

As previously stated, there were thirteen kids in the Tabor household. Hershel was the oldest, then Daddy. At the risk of losing you in a list of begets, which everyone either speed reads through or skips all together, I do feel it necessary to give you the dynamics of the family. The children were born in the order as follows: Hershel in 1922; Daddy, aka Marshall, in 1924; Christine, 1926; Willene, 1928; Mattie, 1929; James, 1931; Vera, 1933; Paul, 1934; Helen, 1936; Pauline, 1938; Margie, 1940; JoAnn, 1942; and last but not least, Raymond, 1943.

Busy Grandma.

Daddy explained that the tensions in the community were rising each day with every news report. He explained, "As I stood in the living room just outside the kitchen doorway, I heard the back door slam. James came runnin' in. He was about ten or eleven at the time, his footsteps thumping hard on the wood floor as he ran up to Mom and said, "Momma! Vera and Helen are sayin' Hitler's comin' to get us. Is that true? I told 'em it wasn't. It ain't true, is it, Ma? I can give him a thing or two, and Hershel and Marshall can take care of him too, right?" He said it with his fists curled up as if he was ready for a fight.

I can only imagine how invincible his big brothers seemed to young James at the time.

"It seemed that no matter who you were or how old you were, all everybody talked about was the war and Hitler," Daddy explained. "It was the topic of pretty much every conversation, and if you weren't talkin' about it, it didn't mean you weren't thinkin' about it. The youngest ones understood just enough to keep 'em from sleepin' good, I reckon."

He looked at me rather seriously. "The more adults whisper and try to hide worries from kids, the more the kids imagine the worst."

I believe that is a basic knowledge he and Mom understood emphatically.

"I walked into the kitchen just in time to see Mom put her bowl down and stop what she was doin'." He continued, "She leaned over and looked James straight in the eyes and said, 'Now, James, don't you worry none. We're miles away from that war, a whole ocean even. We're just trying to help those poor people that need us. Hitler don't care nothin' about coming here. It's nothin' for you to worry about. Besides, you know the Lord is watchin' over us, now don't ya?' James looked her in the eye and said, 'Yes, Momma. I knew it weren't true.'"

As he stared off into the distance, he said, "I remember clear how the house got real quiet as we all took in her words. I hadn't noticed Vera and Helen had come in the back door. I looked up and met their eyes, seein' plain the worry and fear that was still there." He lowered his head and said, "I made a silent promise to not let Hitler come anywhere near my family."

Driving back home that evening, I thought of my own little boys. I cannot imagine seeing them march off to war. I pray it never happens. Walking into my house, I went to them and hugged and kissed their sweet cheeks and said a silent prayer.

CHAPTER 2

Let Me Introduce You to Ruby Kerley, aka Momma

My mother loved music: Patsy Cline, Hank Williams, Kay Star. She loved being on a stage. When she was growing up, she said that every Saturday night, she, Granny and Pa (that's what I have always called her parents), and sometimes her brothers, Hubert and Herbert, might join in with their guitars or fiddles. Yes, that really was their weird names, and no, they were not twins. The community folks took turns going to one or another's house. All the partyers would carry the furniture out into the yard from the biggest room in the house and set up the room as a dance floor. They often played their fiddles or guitars, and sang until the sun came up.

Pa purchased a big upright piano for my mom when she turned eighteen. It now sits in my house as a reminder of one of her most memorable birthdays. She taught herself how to play it. Pa said he always got a kick out of Momma. I have reason to believe his only daughter brought him a great deal of joy. He had said she couldn't do anything without singing. She washed dishes and sang, washed the clothes and sang, and if she could, she'd spend her days singing and playing her instruments and writing songs.

The vision in my head looks similar to a Disney movie.

My grandparents were very protective of her for good reason, I'd have to say. Unfortunately, it was to the point of not allowing her to follow her dreams. My Pa had said something along the lines of, "The world of entertaining for a livin' is not a suitable one for a woman. People will think your morals are bad."

I am sure he just could not allow her to be out in the world on her own. In his mind, either he or a good husband would have to protect her. Times were very different then. Women were never supposed to be on their own. They went from the protection of a father to the protection of a husband. One might even be able to exchange that word *protection* to *control* in some cases. However, my mother was called Ruby Red for more reasons than just her hair color. Her attitude could also be really bright red as well. I think I have even seen flames a time or two. One particular time when those flames were flying was when a couple of guys in high school jumped my brother Larry. Momma had the ringleader backed up to a wall fearing for his life. He was actually very lucky to walk away with all his hair still on his head instead of in her hands. All I can say is, woe be unto any man who tried that control thing. Which, to my knowledge, Daddy had no interest in doing. He was a more "you be you and I will be me, and we can still be us just fine" kind of guy.

I had walked in as Mom was folding laundry. I picked up a towel and carefully folded it as she had taught me to. According to her, there was only one way.

I remembered her saying, "Your Pa would not allow me to be on my own for fear of what people would think. I would tell him that no one thought badly of many other female artists that were performing and seemingly independent." She had sounded *resigned*.

"Mom," I started, "I know you always wanted a career in music, right?" Having heard this many times, I knew the answer. I just wanted to hear, from her, why she had not chosen to pursue that dream.

I picked up another piece of laundry and continued folding.

She looked up with a surprised expression. After a moment's pause, she began, "I did, yes, dream of being a performer. You know, your Pa would not have approved of such a thing." She looked up at me.

"Yes, I guess so. I don't understand why you didn't do it anyway. After you were an adult, you didn't have to stick around, did you?" I asked.

She smiled and said, "Well, it's not that simple." Then she seemed to lighten a bit for a second, recalling, "After Connie was born, me and your Granny and Pa were invited to perform on the *Cas Walker Show*." She was smiling proudly. "They even offered me a contract to join the show as a regular performer."

"Really?" I said excitedly. "Mom, that's a big deal!"

She agreed with a nod of her head, "Yes, at that time, it was." Then sounding somewhat defeated again, she said, "It just wasn't meant to be. By that time, I had five kids at home. Connie was just little." She smiled. "I couldn't imagine not being with my babies every day. Not being here if one got sick. Taking that job would have meant a lot of time away from home. I wouldn't be able to kiss my babies' cheeks every night. That would *not* work," she said with an emphasis on *not*.

I smiled with understanding. After all, I have four of my own. Then I asked, "Can you tell me more about what your life was like when you were young, what the world was like for you then?"

She paused just a moment and then replied, "Well, your Granny spent more time in bed with headaches than out. That left the housework and cooking to me. I would have to run her food, water, headache pills…" She stopped and turned her head a little sideways. "I used to have to push a stool up to the stove to reach it when I first started doing all the cooking. I was scared of most of the farm animals, so working inside suited me just fine. Dad didn't like leavin' her alone, so we tried to make sure one of us was always there if she needed us. Especially on her bad days.

"I remember when we first moved to Crossville from Ohio." I could see the longing in her expression as she talked about living in the city. "It seemed so lonely and desolate here. Nothing but trees!" she explained. "But Dad saw the Depression was getting worse for people in the cities, so we moved," she said while shrugging her shoulders. "We had lived here before, when I was very small. I didn't remember that much about it. Dad used to joke and say I saw a 'booger' behind every tree, and he was right!" We both chuckled. Mom is still afraid of the woods.

I had watched her many times sing and play her guitar, sometimes the piano, and I had no doubt she was as good as anyone I had seen on *Hee Haw* or the Grand Ole Opry. We sat silently, folding each garment, washcloth, and towel for just a moment. Then pushing further, I asked more pointedly, "So what made you choose Daddy?" I have to say, I was a little nervous. What I wanted to hear was that she was madly in love. I was not confident that would be the answer. Not that I questioned she loved him. She sure stuck up for him if anybody, including us, ever said something negative or didn't show the respect we should. But passion? Not sure about that. Ecstatic about what life had given her? Hmmm, good question.

She smiled as she recalled, "Your Pa would always ask, 'Ruby, will Marshall be coming over today?' Unsure of why he was asking, I'd just say, 'Not sure, Dad. He *has* been coming a lot lately.'" She paused and gave a *look*. "Daddy liked him," she continued. "'He's a good boy. Good family. You could do worse, ya know,' he would say. I remember looking at him quizzically. 'What do you mean do worse?' I had asked.

"He said, 'You know, he really likes you. He's not just comin' over here to hang out with me. You'll be finishing school soon. What do you plan to do after that?' I realized I did not have an answer to that question. 'Well, I don't know,' I had responded. In truth, I had dreamed of doing things like going back to the city, but as far as actually planning, or even thinking it all the way through…" Her voice trailed off.

"Then I asked him if he was tryin' to get rid of me." She laughed. "I asked, very seriously, who would cook and clean for him and Mom? I sewed all the clothes and canned all the food! 'What would become of you?' I remember asking. He just grinned and said, 'Honey, we can take care of ourselves. Don't worry about us. It's time for you to live your life. I want you to be happy.'"

A more serious expression replaced the smile on her face when she recalled, "I thought about that and really wasn't sure. What did I want out of life? Marshall was the most handsome boy I had ever seen."

Well, that's a positive, I thought with some relief.

She gave me a sweet smile, saying, "All the girls were jealous that he seemed to like me. I was quite surprised myself. Truth was, I had never considered the idea, or maybe I just didn't expect to live long enough to have a future."

My heart sank.

She went on. "When I started school, I only weighed twenty-four pounds. I was so underweight I was closer to the size of a two-year-old. I heard the adults talking about my weak heart. They actually thought I couldn't hear them. Or maybe they thought I was too young to understand. I knew well who they were talking about when they said 'She will never live to be an adult' or 'Probably won't last much longer.' Those words were whispered often in school and the doctors' offices."

I must have had a rather pitiful expression as she explained, "I got used to it." She shrugged her shoulders. "I guess that's why no one said anything whenever I got tired at school. I would crawl up in the teacher's lap and take a nap."

Well, there's a benefit, I guess.

"Sometimes they would play music and set me on top of the desk, and I would do the Charleston and teach the other kids how to dance."

Perhaps that was when she fell in love with being on a stage.

"The teachers were not worried about me getting an education. I knew why. I don't remember being scared…or worried."

I caught the furrow in her brow. I realized she had learned early on in life how to put on a brave face and flash that bright smile.

Then she took a deep breath and straightened as if gathering her courage, something she had perfected at this point. Then she said, "All of a sudden, I was an adult and was expected to move on in life…plan a future. It would have been nice to move back to the city. I had not thought of much else. Of course, I had not considered being able to leave Dad and Mom, with Mom being sick so much either."

Then there was an obvious shift in her thoughts as she said, "I always loved being at the Tabors' house. It was full of people and had a lot going on. Ours was very quiet in comparison. When I first went into their house, all I saw was shoes lined up and on top of each other as we walked in. I had never seen so many shoes! Of course, my two brothers were away in college. Dad insisted they further their education. I was a bit jealous I didn't get to go. At that time, education for girls was not deemed as important as boys. I decided right then and there I would make sure my girls as well as my boys would have the same opportunities. A lot of the girls I went to school with had already dropped out, married, and were having families of their own. I wasn't ready to do that. I really wanted to finish high school. However, it was getting harder and harder with Mom being so sickly."

My grandmother had been bitten by a rattlesnake while working in the garden. It wasn't the sole cause of her health issues but certainly was a major contributor. She had always been prone to migraine headaches that could often be debilitating.

"Then all of a sudden, here was your Pa ready to marry me off. I wondered what he was thinking," I heard her say. "Maybe he thought he was holding me back."

We sat on the edge of her bed among the stacks of folded towels and washcloths as she continued, "I remember, as Dad and I were having this conversation about my future, we both heard the familiar *clop*, *clop* of a horse's hooves. In spite of not really wanting to, I felt my heart skip a beat. Marshall always looked so handsome sitting up on that horse with a white cowboy hat on. I thought he looked like Roy Rogers!" A smile crept across her face. "That day, though, the closer he got, I saw the look on his face, and my heart dropped. I knew something was wrong. I remember running up to him and asking, 'What is it? What's wrong? Is someone hurt?' The words tumbled out of my mouth.

"He stepped down off his horse, hanging his head low like he couldn't look me in the eyes. He paused before choking out, 'Hershel's been called.'"

My mom's eyes teared up as she remembered the story. "It wasn't unexpected. We all knew it was comin'. Yet it still felt like we had been hit in the chest with a ball bat. I remember him saying, 'He leaves to go to training soon. Looks like they will be sending him to Europe, most likely.' Oh, blasted war! I reached out and hugged him tightly. At that point, my heart hurt for him. I knew how close he and Hershel were, but I was silently relieved it was not him, at least not yet. But then he took the rug right out from under me by announcing, 'I'm goin' in too. I'm going to try and catch up with him, at least soon as I can.'

"I remember half shouting, 'But you have to be eighteen! You're not eighteen yet. You can't go!' I had thought I had more time. Then he just held me back at arm's length, looked at me very seriously, and said, 'I can get in early. It's going to happen anyway. You know that. I have to go.' Then he gave me that grin of his, the one that melted hearts all over Cumberland County, and as much as I hated to admit it, mine too."

Well, that was certainly the romance I had hoped to hear, but I could not stop the welling in my eyes.

Then she explained, "I just stood there, unable to say anything for a while, tryin' to figure out what was wrong with me. I hadn't realized, until then, just how I felt about him."

Mom said she and Daddy got to spend almost every evening sitting out on the front porch, either his or hers. Of course, there were more family get-togethers with the Kerleys and the Tabors than usual. Other families came too. The community pulled together well in those times. There were several young men who came of age and were called off to war. It seemed the population of Winesap and Vandever dropped nearly in half. No family was left unscathed.

Daddy enlisted, lying about his age. They must have known his papers were tampered with, but the military was so desperate, they were known to overlook such technicalities. Men were doing it by the dozens every time another horror story about Hitler's activities came through their little radio speakers.

The last night before he left for Fort Oglethorpe, Georgia, he vowed to write his Ruby a letter every chance he got. Momma said the rest of the conversation was a blur as far as she could remember.

The next thing she knew, he was up on that horse, riding away for the last time before leaving for boot camp. All she could feel was her heart breaking in two. When he was out of sight, she broke down.

"I tried to calm the tears that were gulping out of my body," she explained. "I was talking to myself, saying, 'This was *not* what I wanted! I wanted to finish school and go back to the city and become a singer and *not* this, NOT THIS!"

She had fresh tears rolling down her cheeks. I sat silently, anxiously. "Then, I remember Dad had appeared from nowhere and was holding me as I screamed and cried. 'Oh, Daddy, oh, Daddy' was all I could say." She went on, the sadness raw in her voice. "Our house was very quiet over the next few weeks. The music had been taken right out of my heart."

Suddenly, she seemed to perk up a bit, recalling, "Every day, I ran to the mailbox as soon as it was delivered. Every night I lay in the floor on my stomach, feet in the air, writing letters to him. He must have written as soon as he got to Georgia, and he was probably met with a letter from me as soon as he arrived. It wasn't long before I received the first letter. I remember my hands trembling as I took it out of the mailbox. I tore it open, running back into the house. I was yelling, 'Daddy, Daddy, I got a letter from Marshall!' He had carried a pile of wood in and was stoking the fire. He looked up and gave me a warm and *approving* smile.

"I knew for sure then he really liked Marshall. I decided at that moment, given the opportunity, I was going to marry that man. Then, as if he'd read my mind all the way from Georgia, there it was. Simple and sweet."

She stood up and went to her chest of drawers. She opened the top one and pulled out a very old, obviously aged envelope. She smiled sweetly and handed it to me. I reached my hand out, slowly taking the envelope. Carefully, as if it were a fragile treasure, I opened the flap and pulled out the one-page letter inside. Unfolding it as if it might disintegrate in my hand, with tear-filled eyes, and between sniffles, I read aloud,

> *Dear Ruby,*
>
> *I am all settled in at Ft. Oglethorpe. Just got here but already homesick. I hope you are all doing well. If you can, please check on Momma and the kids. I miss you, and I really miss Ole Joe. I am sure Christine and Momma will see to it he gets took care of.*

We both chuckled. It was Daddy all right. Being the romantic he was, he missed his horse the most, it sounded like.

"Sometimes he is really aggravating," Mom said, chuckling through fresh tears.

I started again,

> *I know I am not supposed to ask this in a letter, but I have a*

question for you. A real serious one. I will be coming back after basic for a few weeks. What I'd like to say is, well, what if we got married and you could come back with me? We could live in the housing on base while I wait for my orders. When I get them and ship out, you could go back home and wait for me. I might just be able to get through this if I know I have you to come back home to.

Love,
Marshall

I looked up in time to see a smile on her face. She said, "I had to admit, it wasn't the most romantic proposal, *maybe*." We both knew Daddy was a man of few words, but what he said held meaning. "It was Marshall, true enough." She continued, "If he said it, you could count on it." Then she repeated, "I might just be able to get through this if I know I have you to come home to." We both felt the weight of those words.

Then she said, "After I read the letter, I handed it over to your Pa. I distinctly recall him eyeing me over his glasses with a wrinkled forehead. He never said a word, but I saw the question. I smiled and said, 'Daddy, I think I'm getting married.'"

He gave me a warm smile back, and that said all I needed to hear.

CHAPTER 3

Finding Hershel

"I couldn't tell ya how long we had been walkin'. We had landed on the beaches of Normandy right after the initial invasion. I guess our brains were numb after seeing the devastation. We just marched in silence. I couldn't stop thinkin' about Hershel. For miles, all you could hear was the crunch of boots. I knew I would not be able to rest until I could find out if he was okay. That's when I started lookin' for anybody that might have information. If I saw any other troop or Red Cross station, I would ask if they had a record of him. If he hadn't made it, somebody would know. All I could think about when we pulled in was, 'How could anybody have survived this?' There had been over 5,000 ships and 160,000 troops sent to push their way through. The only chance we stood of winnin' the war was getting control of France. We had all heard the rumors, over 10,000 dead. The first bunch didn't stand a chance. They knew it too. Steppin' right out into the line of fire."

He looked at me intently to see if I understood exactly what had taken place. I wondered, *What kind of strength did those men have? Where could it have possibly come from? Did they hesitate at all? Perhaps they clung to pictures in their minds of girlfriends, wives, children, or parents?*

Then he said so softly, like he could barely get the words out, "Hershel had been right in the middle of it." He choked. "There was so much broken and busted-up wood on the water you could almost walk across it. All those ships were just blown apart. I didn't hold much hope at first," he said, lowering his head, attempting to once again hide the raw emotion that time could not heal. "Then I heard your grandpa's voice in my head," he explained, "readin' from the Bible on the front porch, 'Even though I walk through the valley of the shadow of death, I'll fear no evil.'"

I realized I had never actually heard Daddy quote scripture before. At least not in a traditional way. Then again, maybe he had in his own way, of course. Like when he'd say, "Aw, don't take everything to heart. It'll work itself out in the end," aka "Be still and know that I am God" or "You ort [yes, that's a word] not treat a feller that way [meaning unjustly or unkindly] just 'cause he's different," aka "Love your neighbor as yourself," and of course, "Now, Sonda [it took him years to figure out my name], you ort not do that," aka "Children, obey your parents." Those words coming from him carried more weight than you know.

Not that I was a terrible kid or anything, not really. Probably only a hair away from perfect by most standards. Maybe. Sort of.

Looking up again, he said, "I decided I wasn't gonna let myself give up hope just yet. Some made it. He might've. I just had to tell myself that over and over until I could find out for sure. So I set out to do just that. When we would come across Red Cross stations, other troops, or *anybody* friendly, I'd ask them if they had any record of a Hershel Tabor. If the answer was no, I figured that was a good sign. Had he died, surely the Red Cross would know. Whatever way I could, I'd find out. I could hear Momma say, 'Prayer changes things.' Figured I might as well give it try."

Staring out the window directly in front of his chair, he said rather whimsically, "I could just see them all, Dad and Mom, all the kids, gathered around on the front porch. Paul and James would be sittin' on the steps, baby Jo in Mom's lap. Dad readin' from the Bible like always. I figured they just might be doin' that right at that moment. Could be about the right time a whole other world away. I could almost smell home from whatever would be cookin' in the kitchen to Ole Joe and manure in the barn." He turned to look at me and grinned. "Never thought I'd miss that so much. I knew I'd never take it for granted again if I got the chance."

It certainly explained why Daddy never was a traveler. Mom and I were just the opposite. We traveled everywhere between Jekyll Island to Alaska. Daddy never minded at all as long as he got to stay home.

"Were you able to find out, before you got back home at least, what had happened to Hershel?" I asked.

"Yeah, I did. It wasn't too long before I got the opportunity to talk to one of the guys in his troop."

"Really?" I asked surprised.

"We were marchin' along when we heard the sounds of a heated battle not far in the distance. We all jerked to attention and looked at the sergeant. He was quick to start calling orders with a hand in the air, lettin' us know how to proceed. We weren't sure at that point if we'd be comin' in front of or behind the enemy. We followed his orders and did what we was told, movin' in as low as we could go. At that moment, I decided I would not want that man's job, directly responsible for each one of us. That'd be a right heavy load to bear. Whether you knew what to do or not, you had to convince everyone you did. Morale was a hard thing to keep up and more important than you know. Our boys went in with no hope at all. I remembered Hershel sayin' we didn't stand a chance. After we stormed the beaches of France, though, things had started lookin' up. Not that you could tell by what we had seen so far. There was dead animals, butchered with bullets, layin' all over the place. Trees were just shredded. Any buildings and homes we'd come across were mostly destroyed. There were times, you literally were stepping over human bodies…" His voice trailed off.

I silently shuddered as this vision took form. Thing is, often he did not have to speak his visions into my head. They would show up unexpectedly, without a word spoken. This often happened when we were nowhere near each other. Weird, I know. Even though I lived a few hours away, there were times that I would get to where I could not breath. I would panic. My poor husband would rush me to the doctor or nearest ER. I felt like I was suffocating and could not get air into my lungs. I was put on inhalers and various medications. One doctor said I had asthma. Later, I would find out that Daddy had been rushed to the doctor or nearest ER at the same time and was unable to breath. He would also panic. He actually had emphysema, an easily diagnosable and understandable reason to be short of breath. When I figured out my episodes coincided with his and somehow my body was just feeling his pain, instead of panicking and running to a doctor, I learned to calm myself down and pray. I prayed for Daddy, knowing he was the one in trouble. Then I'd call home, rather than waiting to be called, to find out how he was. I took myself off all the medication and especially those nasty inhalers. See, I told you it was weird.

"Once we got to where the battle was," I heard him saying, "I saw the insignia on the shoulders of the other troop across the way. It was the same as Hershel's. I told the fellers beside me I was gonna make my way over to talk to one of their men. They tried to get me to stay put, but I didn't want to miss the opportunity. Hard tellin' when I'd get another'n," he explained.

"So I just stayed low and made my way over. Dust was flyin' and bullets hittin' all around, makin' it hard to focus. I finally came up on one of the guys from his troop and crawled up next to him and asked if he knew Hershel. He nodded and kept firin'. I was firin' too and was half afraid one of us was gonna get hit before I could get my answer. So I asked real quick if he knew what happened to him or where he was at. I half expected him to say he was around there somewhere. I looked as best I could, but it was hard to make out any faces. Of course, we was spread out in a purdy wide circle." He paused a moment and then went on, "It seemed like it took 'em forever before he

finally answered and said Hershel had been injured
and sent home. Said he'd gotten his arm blown off."

"His arm?" I squealed.

"Yeah, that's what he said. We had 'em outnumbered pretty good, so they finally gave up. We took
a few prisoners. When I got back to where my troop
was, the first person I saw was Roscoe. He and I stuck
close together. We met at boot camp and were from
near the same area of Tennessee. He was a big ole
burly feller, rough as a cobb. I think we gave each
other a connection to home. In the downtime, we
could talk about the Tennessee mountains we were
both familiar with. So we tried to keep an eye on
each other. Roscoe asked, 'Marshall, did you find
anything out about your brother?' I said, 'Yeah, he
got sent home!' I was real relieved, grinnin' ear to ear,
I reckon. Then I said, 'He got his arm blown off.'
Roscoe and the other fellers standin' around looked
at me real odd-like, so I said, 'Well, I guess that part
maybe don't sound so good, but he'll be okay, and
he's home.' I was still grinnin', considerin'…"

"But he told you Hershel's arm was blown off?"
I asked again, incredulously.

"Yeah, I didn't find out until I got home that is
was just part of his hand."

"Wow. That sounds pretty awful," I said.

"At the time, it didn't sound nearly as awful as it
could have been. Just knowin' he was home safe and
not comin' back was enough for me."

"Yeah, I suppose so." I tried to imagine how I would feel if one of my brothers or sisters were in such a situation. First, witnessing the horrible destruction they had been faced with, and then the not knowing. The searching. The hoping. The praying. I certainly understood the relief in spite of the injury. "So were you only in France, or did you have to go to other countries?" I asked.

"No, we traveled all over. We liberated some of the concentration camps. That was something I could never understand. The prisoners looked like walking skeletons they were so starved. It was dead of winter, and they were outside, naked, frostbit. How a feller could treat another'n like that is beyond me."

He choked again, trying to describe the death camps. "We had taken control of one and stood outside the fence when several of 'em asked if we'd cut the fence and let 'em out so they could get to their families. We were told not to so they could process them out and keep a record, but I couldn't say no. They had been through so much already. So we did. It was the most heartbreakin' thing I've ever seen."

He was struggling to talk. I was struggling to listen. The truth is, I didn't need him to go into a lot of details. I have seen enough footage and pictures taken by my uncle Hubert. He was a photographer for the military. He went in to get pictures and proof of the atrocities. He had photos of piles of bodies.

He also had close-ups showing markings and tags on some for identification.

I had the privilege of visiting the Holocaust Memorial in Jerusalem. It was the most painful thing I have ever done. When you take your first step into the Children's Memorial, the first thing you see are pictures of sweet, young faces whose lives were taken brutally for no reason at all. There was a skinny little boy with blond hair that reminded me of my youngest. He looked maybe six. Those pictures were suspended in the air inside a glass display surrounded by one million candles that were kept lit by volunteers in remembrance of the one million children that died by the hand of a prejudice I find impossible to understand. As you make your way past this huge display, you see pictures and letters framed on the walls. One I remember distinctly was of a family about to be executed. They were lined up along the edge of a large hole dug into the ground that would serve as a mass grave. Gunmen lined up the opposite side ready to fire. The mom had her arms around three little ones. The dad was holding a young boy, perhaps four or five years old, pointing toward heaven. You could almost hear what he was saying, "Don't worry, we are going there, it will be okay." The little boy looked so scared yet trying hard to be brave. He was listening intently and looking heavenward to where he and his family would be soon. I'm not sure I can tell you much after that.

I remember exiting the building on the other side. The sunlight felt so warm. I raised my face toward it and closed my eyes, hoping to calm my trembling body. I must have looked like I needed help. An elderly lady I had never seen before walked up and put her arms around me. I broke down and cried convulsively on her shoulder. When I was finally able to speak, we introduced ourselves. She explained she had been a prisoner in one of the camps. My brain was numb, and I wish I could tell you what all she said. What I do recall was her sweet smile and comforting voice. We talked until I was able to get my feet working properly, and I headed toward the exit.

Before leaving, I squeezed her tightly, thanking her and letting her know how glad I was to have met her. As the tour bus pulled away, what had been a very chatty bunch was now totally silent. There were no words. Or perhaps, they were just lodged in our throats.

CHAPTER 4

Ruby and Her Encounter with Ole Joe

The house was quiet. Daddy and Granny were both asleep. Mom was sitting in her rocker while sipping a glass of wine. I poured myself one as well and went in to sit in the chair beside her. She just sat there quietly. No TV or music. She was staring out the big window into the night lit up brightly by a full moon and clear, sparkling sky.

"What ya thinkin'?" I asked, knowing full well all the talk about the past with Daddy had stirred more memories for her also.

She raised her glass and took a drink before setting it down softly. I watched her closely. Her face still looked very much as it always had. Somehow, she had escaped the weathered and wrinkled skin that usually went with her age. She had always been adamant about protecting her face from the sun and, of course, taking good care of her skin. She often made her own skin care products, which she used religiously. Obviously, skin care companies would have done well to get her recipes. Natural and organic were her key words long before anyone else thought them important. I remember her warning us to never use baby powder or talcum powder of any sort on ourselves or our babies. She had said it would cause cancer. This was back in the seventies, something that would not become common knowledge for years. I wondered how she knew that. You never really had to ask for her opinion. You would get it long before you knew you needed it. She lived up to her name, Ruby Red. She had red hair, all right, but that is not what the *red* actually referred to. She was a 5'3" stick of dynamite. The red on top was just a warning label.

She made and often designed our clothes growing up. I remember when I was only fifteen years old, I asked to go to modeling school in Atlanta. Whatever made me think I could be a model, I have no idea. Apparently, Momma and Daddy either did not have the heart to be honest with me, or they quite possibly saw me through the eyes of love that covers a multitude of shortcomings.

I stayed with my uncle Hugh and his wife, Aunt Rita, who lived in Atlanta. I attended the fabulous Barbizon Modeling School. Mom and I designed all my outfits to take. I was required to have a sporty, a casual, and a formal for a photo shoot. I drew them on paper. She made the patterns and sewed them into reality.

After a bit of measuring and cutting and fittings that always resulted in my body feeling like a pin cushion, there were times I was pretty sure if I drank a glass of water, it would spew out like a water sprinkler. I suddenly had my new wardrobe. I could honestly say I had the most well-made, beautifully designed, and classy-looking outfits in the class.

I remember being asked by students and instructors alike where I had shopped. I sheepishly answered, "My mother made them." I was surprised at their reaction. They seemed impressed. I was shocked! I had worried about fitting in when I could not afford buying my wardrobe from a big department store like I assumed the other girls had. Even at school, I was a bit shy about my wardrobe. I wore whatever Mom made, for the most part. It was years before I was able to wear jeans like everyone else. When I went to my twenty-year class reunion, we were reintroducing ourselves to old classmates, and one fellow said to me, "Oh, I remember you!" He then described me in a way that left me totally speechless. He said, "You were the classy girl that wore suits and scarves." Isn't it strange how we see ourselves, but if we get a peek at how others see us, it is sooooooo *totally* different than we ever imagined? All this time, I thought I was the weird kid whose mother wouldn't buy her jeans. *Classy* was never a word that came to mind.

I took a good look at this woman whom I'd always called Mom. I carefully weighed the assumptions I had made about her. I had *assumed* she had always been exactly as I have always seen her—never young, never vulnerable, never not completely in control.

I watched as the reel seemed to play across her mind, going back, back, and further back in time, pictures and emotions long past springing back to life. "One day I do recall very clearly," she spoke suddenly. "I was looking at the new dress I was working on for Christine." A warm smile crossed her face. "I remember thinking it was coming together quite nicely. It was a simple A-line with a rounded collar and small shoulder pads. I always thought big shoulder pads made women look too masculine." She looked at me seriously while sipping her wine.

"It was a winter dress with a matching cloak. I had made the dress with three-quarter-lengthed sleeves. I had found a pair of white gloves for her on sale at Hill's department store in town. I was really excited about helping Ms. Tabor with her project for the girls and was finishing the detailed stitching on the sleeves when I heard that familiar sound. Before, there would have been a rider on top, but that day, he came alone."

She trailed off dreamily and tilted her head slightly with a bit of a grin. "It was a *clop, clop,* and whinny." Momma shook her head. "That poor horse," she said wholeheartedly. "He escaped his confines and found his way through the woods to my house almost daily after Marshall had gone off to war."

"He was looking for Daddy, wasn't he?" I asked.

"I'm sure he was." Then she stated, "It was no short distance either! Perhaps eight to ten miles by car, a little shorter through the woods. Marshall had cut a trail that maybe took off three or four miles, at most."

I am sure my eyes widened. The very thought he had cut a trail through the woods between their houses warmed my heart. In this neck of the woods, that was the epitome of romantic.

She continued, "Your Pa was at the sawmill working. Mom was sleeping, and as much as I hated to, I was the only one around to try and make sure Ole Joe was securely put away and didn't get lost or hurt." She visibly shook as she said, "I shuttered at the thought! You know how afraid I am of horses!"

I giggled a little. *Everyone* knew how afraid Momma was of horses. After all these years way out here on this farm, *that* had never changed. We had all tried at one point or another to get her to ride with us and perhaps just warm up to them but to no avail.

"I looked out at that horse," she explained with a very sad and forlorn expression. "He was just standing there, looking so solemn. I noticed he had the same expression I had seen so many times before on his master's face. Perhaps they were just two parts of the same soul." She visibly squared her shoulders a bit before going on. "Somehow, I mustered up the courage to go out there. I put on my boots and coat and walked quickly out the door before I could change my mind," she said with determination.

Momma took another slow sip of her wine as if mustering up courage at the very thought. "For a second, I thought about going to the sawmill and getting your Pa to come help but decided that was not practical. Mom was sick again, and I didn't want her to wake up and find me gone. Walking him back to the Tabors' house was definitely not an option. The only choice I had, I decided, was to put him in our fence with Dad's cow. We had a small shed for shelter. I could give him some of the cow's feed, get him locked in where he would at least be safe."

Smiling again, she said, "So I took a deep breath and kept repeating to myself, 'I can do this. I can do this.' Then I walked out the door quietly and tiptoed across the porch and down the steps, careful not to scare him off. I distinctly remember whispering to myself, 'Just walk quietly, quietly.' As I crept closer, all of a sudden, he whinnied real loud and huffed a big cloud of smoke right in front of my face! I screamed and fell backward right on my behind with a jolt!"

I could not hold back a laugh.

She became very animated as she continued her description. "I jumped up real quick and looked around, hoping no one saw me!" She turned her head left to right.

We were both laughing at this point.

"When I turned to Ole Joe, he was lookin' at me like, 'What's wrong with you?' I'd swear he had the oddest expression on his face. Then he just stood there still as a statue, watching, as I picked myself up and dusted off my behind. I was shaking all over but determined not to let that animal get the best of me. So I took another deep breath, stood up straight, hoping my 5'3" stature would seem at least a little intimidating, and slowly took a small step forward," she explained.

She was whispering again now, her previous joyful mood had dissipated into a more serious tone. "He just stood without moving, watching me intently."

I watched while she raised her hand up in the air as if that horse stood before her at that very moment. "I laid my hand on his nose," she explained softly, wrinkling her brow a bit as if a question skittered across her thoughts, and said in a rather singsongy voice, "I had not realized how soft a horse's nose was until that moment."

I sat quietly, absorbed in her story.

"I put my hand on his head. We were looking at each other directly in the eyes," she gasped slightly, "when I saw," she paused a moment, "*something.*"

I thought for a second she was going to make me ask what it was she saw. I leaned forward, closing the distance between us. Just as I opened my mouth to form the question, she began. "I saw your daddy," she said in a quiet but firm tone.

I was confused. "You mean he was home? Walking up the driveway?"

"No, I looked into that horse's eyes. They were big and brown and deep as the sea, just like Marshall's." She grinned slightly. "For a moment, I was completely paralyzed. I felt slightly faint, but I would not let Ole Joe see that. I stepped up as close as I could get, right up to his face, and just stood there, staring. I couldn't believe it." She paused to take a short breath as I waited on the edge of my seat. Then, as if entranced, she explained, "As clearly as I see you right now, I saw him walking from behind. He had on his combat uniform and helmet. I suppose it could have been the back of any soldier, except I could tell by the way he walked and moved, it was Marshall. Then he turned and looked straight back at me."

She turned to face me and looked me directly in the eyes, to make sure I understood. "Like, he could see me too. He smiled...*right* at me," she said adamantly. She paused a moment, I think, to see if I could comprehend what she was saying.

I nodded slightly.

She went on, "I'm not sure how long I stood there before I realized I was holding my breath. I gulped in a cold breath of air as he disappeared. Just like that." She made a slow and silent snap of her fingers in the air. She lowered her head and laid her hands gently on her lap.

I couldn't respond, so I sat very still, quietly waiting for her to continue, at her own pace.

"I stood there, searching, looking intently, hoping he'd come back," she said rather sadly, "until I felt the tears freeze on my cheek that I had not realized were falling. I took another big breath of cold air and shook myself back to reality. I remember thinking I had to get 'hold of myself. I might have even said so out loud to Ole Joe, I suppose. He was the only one around." She grinned again slightly and shrugged her shoulders.

"I was just trying to breathe, move, before I froze to the ground. After regaining my composure, I tried to sound like I was the boss." She tilted her head a little and gave me a look that said *that* part was probably questionable. She said, "In the firmest sounding voice I could muster, I said, 'Now, Joe, you cannot be out here just running around on your own. Marshall wants us to take good care of you, you understand?' At that point, I had lost control of the tears spilling down my cheeks. I wondered then what that horse did understand. Adults are prone to think children do not understand their conversations, secrets, and whispers. I know they are very wrong. 'Maybe we're wrong about you too, huh, Joe?' I asked him. I reached out and touched his head and pled, trying not to sound too desperate, remembering what Marshall had said about how all animals sense fear and then react to it. They have to know you are the boss. 'Take control,' he had said, so I gave it my best shot. 'Follow me, Joe,' I demanded firmly."

I realized I was holding my breath, as if somehow I, too, could spook that poor horse.

"I kept my hand laid on his neck. I did not have a rope or a bridal, you understand," she said, giving me her look. "Much to my surprise, he followed along very easily. I led him to the gate, carefully opening it. He walked right in beside me." She sounded amazed.

A twinkle of pride appeared in her eyes as she recalled that particular memory. She had for a moment faced a fear and encountered *something* very close to magical.

She continued, "I gave him some feed and filled the water trough. As I started back into the house, I realized I was still shaking. Whether it was from the experience or the cold, I was not sure. My heart was

still beating rather rapidly, so I decided a hot cham-
omile tea was in order. As I removed my coat and
boots, I heard your granny begin to stir. I went into
the kitchen to put a kettle of water on as I heard her
footsteps coming out of her room.

"I turned to ask her if she'd like a cup also,
but when I turned to face her, her widened eyes
and expression stopped me. 'Ruby, are you okay?'
she asked, looking concerned. Then before I could
answer, she said, 'You look like you have seen a ghost!'
I remember saying, 'I think I may have, sort of.' It
came out choked and strained. I was a little worried
I was hallucinating, perhaps even totally losing my
mind. I started to try and just let it pass. I said, 'Oh,
it was nothing.' But Mom wasn't buying that. So I
just said, 'Have a seat by the fireplace. I'll make us a
cup of tea and see if I can explain it.'"

"You told Granny about what you saw?" I asked
curiously. She nodded her head yes. Then I asked,
"What did she think about it?"

"Well, as I recall, after I made myself and Mom
a hot cup of tea, my hands were still trembling and
my teeth were chattering as I carried the cups into the
living room. We sat in side-by-side rockers in front
of a roaring fire. I sat hers down easily on the small
end table between. I asked her how she was feeling.
She said she was some better and the tea was a good
idea. She looked at me quizzically. Obviously, I didn't
have a good poker face. Dad said I wore my feelings

right out there for everyone to see. If I disagreed with something, it showed. If I doubted what I heard, it was obvious. He said not much got past me, and I was sure to have, and speak, my opinion whether it was popular or not."

Momma shrugged her shoulders. "Not so sure that's always a good thing, Suni," she said, looking directly at me before turning her head and taking a deep breath before going on with her story. "I laid a throw across your granny's lap and then mine. We just sat there silently for a few minutes, sipping our tea. I distinctly remember how good it felt warming me from the inside out. Then Mom put her hand on mine 'So, Ruby,' she said, 'is there something you want to talk about? Are you feeling okay?' she asked, concerned.

"I turned to face her directly. I needed to see her reaction as I explained what I had just seen. I felt pretty sure by then, I was not hallucinating or losing my mind. I knew what I saw. I started by asking her if she'd ever seen something, clearly seen something, she couldn't quite understand or explain. At first, she just sat there, looking at me curiously like she was not sure where I was going with this.

"My resolve started to melt a little, but I decided to just describe my vision *exactly* as I had seen it. I started at the beginning and even told her about falling on my butt, embarrassing as that was. Then after, having said it all out loud, with every detail and all the clarity I could put into words, I started to think that maybe I had dreamed the whole thing. 'It was nothing, right?' I remember asking her. I was moving the throw off my lap and starting to get up out of my chair and just leave it at that. It was nothing. Then she reached out and patted my arm and said, 'Have a seat. Let me explain something to you.'"

I smiled slightly and said, "She didn't think it was nothing, did she?" I remembered many stories Granny had told me growing up about odd things that had happened in her life. One of the oddest was she had refused to let a scary, witchy lady deliver Momma when she was born. Everyone in the community was afraid of this woman, including Granny. The woman was very upset that Granny would not allow her to be her midwife and promptly put a curse on Mom. After Mom was born, she did not stop crying. Day and night, Pa and Granny took turns staying up, walking the floors with her. Finally, someone told Granny that in order to break the curse, she had to let Mom soak three diapers good and wet and then burn them. Out of sheer desperation, they followed the lady's orders. After the third diaper was burned, they all slept through the night, peacefully, for the first time in six months.

Momma nodded affirmation and then continued, "Your Granny then said to me in her very own words, 'Do you want to hear a story? A story that has no real explanation that I know of?' I said, 'Oh, Mom,

I know all about the curse and the witchy lady,' but she interrupted me by saying, 'No, I know you know all about that.' I looked at her quizzically as she began, 'Do you want to know how I learned to play the piano?' I admit, I was caught a little off guard for a second and wondered what that had to do with anything. However, I sat in silence and allowed her to continue.

"'One night, I dreamed I was playing this beautiful song that I had never even heard before. I saw each note, felt each ivory key soft on my fingertips. That dream felt as real to me as anything ever had awake,' she said firmly. 'Then, when I woke up, I ran straight to the piano and played just like in my dream, as if I had done it all my life. It was like I suddenly understood each note and its special tune by heart. I've been playing ever since, yet...' She stopped, pointing her finger straight up. 'I had never done so before. Explain that, will you?'

"With raised eyebrows, we both giggled a little. Then she explained she had another little story I might find hard to believe, but it was true nonetheless. 'Have I ever told you about your dad, how we met, I mean?' I thought about it and concluded that no, I had never heard them talk about their young life together. I said, 'Tell me. I'd love to hear it.' With a wry smile, she began to tell me quite seriously that she had met him in a dream as well."

Mom was smiling slightly as she recalled Granny explaining that. "One night, she had another very vivid dream about this tall, skinny fellow. She saw him clearly in her dream, and as she was introduced to him, she heard a voice say, 'This is the man you are going to marry.' A few months after that, a new family moved into the community. They had moved from the valley in Bledsoe County up the Cumberland Plateau. Everyone gathered at their new home to welcome them. She said you could have knocked her over with a feather when she entered and saw the man literally from her dreams. He was 6'4" and skinny as a rail, with thick auburn hair. She had to crane her neck to see his pale face with those high cheekbones and sparkling blue eyes. 'Walter Kerley,' she whispered under her breath as they were introduced for the first [second] time. Her hands trembled as she reached out to shake his. That night, she went to sleep whispering his name into her pillow repeatedly. Your granny told me simply, 'You live long enough, you'll see plenty of things you won't be able to explain. The world is full of surprises.'" She looked at me with a wink.

I found myself sitting on the edge of my chair, mesmerized. "Wow" was the only reaction I could muster.

"Later that night," Mom went on, "I was cooking dinner, only half aware of my movements, deep in thought, as if operating by remote control. I kept thinking about it all, trying to process it. I was hardly aware of what I was doing when I looked at the table completely set with plates and food. I had made a pot of pinto beans, cornbread, mashed potatoes, and fried chicken. It was all ready and waiting for Dad's return. We always sat down to dinner together and discussed the day's events. I was not so sure I wanted to discuss my day with Dad. I remember thinking he might not be quite as understanding as Mom about such strange things. I was not quite sure.

"First thing Dad said as he walked in the door was, 'I see Ole Joe is back.' I looked up at him and said, 'Yeah, poor horse. He's lost without Marshall. I think he keeps trying to find him here.' Daddy replied, 'Looks that way. Did *you* get him put up?' he asked with obvious surprise. In reality, he was not as surprised as I was. 'Yes, as a matter of a fact, I did. Fed and watered him too! Not that I care to make a habit of it, but I can handle things…when I have to.' I didn't want to go into any details if I could avoid it. He'd get a big kick out of it if he had seen the whole fiasco that had bruised by backside. Technically, my pride was probably more bruised than my backside.

"Luckily, Mom was still up for dinner, and we gathered at the table. So often she either ate in bed or didn't eat at all. I wish I could've figured out what caused her headaches to be so debilitating. Doctors said it was a possible form of epilepsy. They gave her medicine for the pain when it got too unbearable. Other than that, there didn't seem to be much any-one could do. It was sweet to watch your Pa with her.

He was always so kind and thoughtful. He tried really hard to take care of her. I often felt sorry for him carrying the burden as he did. I'd worried I could end up being a burden for someone to take care of. That thought felt more like a dreaded shudder. I hoped I would never get to be that needy," she said. "I knew this weak heart of mine was a little like living with a time bomb. I had rather just die of it than be so weak and helpless, always having to be taken care of. I didn't want to do that to Marshall...or my children."

I was surprised to hear that was a worry she had ever had. As long as I could remember, she had taken care of everyone around her, certainly never the other way around.

"I made a mental note as we were eating dinner together that night that my kids would not carry the burden of the family. I wanted them to run and play and be children. I would encourage their dreams, always," I heard her say.

By then I had moved to the couch closer to where she sat and put my hand on hers. "You did that, Mom. We had an amazing childhood."

She nodded with a proud grin and took another sip, replacing the glass on the coaster before continuing. "Later that night, I contemplated the events of that day while washing and putting the dishes away, what I had seen or thought I'd seen and what Mom had said. The world can be very mysterious, I decided."

"Apparently," I reiterated.

"When my head finally hit the pillow that night, I began tossing and turning. Every time I closed my eyes, I saw Ole Joe's big brown eyes, Marshall's sly smile. I could envision him sitting up there on top of Joe's back, looking every bit the regal cowboy. I tried to go to sleep, but all I did was toss and turn. Finally, I jumped up out of bed, put my boots back on, and threw the nearest shawl around my shoulders. For whatever reason, I didn't feel the fear I had before of that big horse. I *needed* to go see him. I wanted to see if *he* was still *there*, or figure out if he ever was. I walked softly across the floor and slowly opened the front door, trying not to make any noises that would disturb Mom and Dad. I was sure they would think I was nuts! Going out in the dark to see a horse was *very* out of character for me." She giggled softly.

I agreed wholeheartedly.

"I headed toward the field and small barn. When I opened the gate, Joe actually turned and walked right up to me. He was probably a little surprised to see me too, I suspect. Easily, I laid my hand on his soft nose again. 'You miss him as much as I do, don't you, boy?' I remember saying. I stood there for a moment, looking in his eyes again to see if there was anything *unusual*. I am not sure how long I had stood there when, suddenly, I noticed the most beautiful white big fluffy snowflakes falling slowly from the sky. I looked up and caught one with my tongue. A flake hit my nose, and I actually felt a little giggle escape. The first snow of the year. I looked at Joe and saw only the loneliness, aching deep in his soul, just like mine. 'Yes, boy, you do understand,' I said. Then again, with as much certainty as I could muster, I said firmly, as if it the words alone would make it so, 'He will be back.' I was patting his head when I heard a noise behind me and almost jumped right out of my skin as I turned to face whatever had come upon me!"

"'What on earth are you doing out here, Ruby?' I heard Dad say. 'You'll catch your death of cold if you're not careful!' he exclaimed. The look on his face betrayed him, though. Yes, he was worried, I know, but some little part of him was proud of me too. I could see it. 'Daddy, you shouldn't sneak up on me like that. You 'bout gave me heart attack!' A quick thought passed through my head that that was not the best analogy. He looked at me very seriously.

"'Don't say that,' he said in a soft whisper like he had just faced his worst fear. It dawned on me that I had never really considered how my heart condition had affected him and Mom, having a child they felt they could lose at any given moment. It made me feel so sorry for them all of a sudden. I looked at Dad straight in the eyes and said more firmly than anything I had ever said to anyone before, 'Those doctors are wrong. I think I have proven that already, and one day I will show them. I will march a line of kids right through their damned offices and show them just how little they know!'

"To my surprise, he smiled. Then he said, 'That's my little Ruby all right! Just don't start cussing on me, or we'll get a bad reputation.' With that, he put his arm around my shoulders and led me back into the warmth of the house. I hadn't realized just how cold I was until we entered. Passing through the door, he turned to go to his and Mom's room. I turned toward mine and said over my shoulder without turning around, 'I love you, Daddy.' I heard a smile behind his quiet reply. 'Good night, baby girl.'

"I laid my head down on my pillow for the second time, quietly singing, 'I wanna be a cowboy's sweetheart,' until I fell asleep."

CHAPTER 5

Shortcuts

I walked into the house to a familiar scene. Daddy sat in front of Mom as she played her guitar and sang a new song she had just written. Judging from the grin on his face and the look he was giving her, it was the best song he had ever heard. She looked up at me, smiling, never missing a beat as I took a seat on the couch across from them.

I knew she had entered a contest with the local chamber to write a song about Crossville. Her song had been chosen in the top 3, and she would be going to their next meeting to sing it for all the members, at which point the winner would be chosen. Daddy assured her sweetly she had this one in the bag. No worries.

SUNI NELSON

Then Mom and I sang "I Want to Be a Cowboy's Sweetheart" as she showed off her yodeling skills. After a bit, Mom decided it was bath and pajama time for her. I looked over at Daddy and said, "Do you need anything?"

Suddenly, he said, "Hey, why don't you get us a shot glass of that moonshine that's on the kitchen counter?"

With widened eyes, I said, "Moonshine?" I expected him to ask for Little Debbie cakes. This was different.

"Yeah," he replied. "It's peach. The feller across the lake brought it over today. I bet it's good."

I giggled a little and said, "Sure," as I got back up and went into the kitchen. I opened the cabinet where the glasses had been kept in perfect order now for forty or maybe fifty years? I question my memory. My sister Carolina had once told Momma she had named each of her drinking glasses and cups. They had to always be put back in their reserved spot. I thought it was nice that some things managed to stay the same. Comforting, somehow.

I pulled out the tiny shot glasses and sat them on the counter. I wondered for a moment if I should pour moonshine like wine, only fill the glass just a bit of the way, or should I fill it since it was such a small glass. *Hmmmmm. Perhaps in this case, less really is more.* So I put what I deemed an appropriate amount of moonshine in the shot glasses and headed back to my interview chair.

I saw that look on his face again. That sad, soulful look. I knew he was remembering something. Perhaps moonshine instead of Little Debbie cakes was a better idea after all. "What's on your mind, Daddy?" I asked a bit sheepishly. I still feared stirring the monster that these memories might possibly raise.

"I was thinkin' about that shipwreck, I guess," he said quietly. Then he visibly shook just a little. "Well, maybe I should start with the hospital first," he said, sounding a bit stronger.

"Hospital?" I repeated with raised eyebrows. Then I added, "Start wherever you want, Daddy... Are you sure you want to do this? If it's too hard, I don't want to—"

I didn't get the question all the way out until he stopped me by putting his hand up. He looked at me very seriously and said, "Yeah, I want to do this." I knew he meant it. I guess after having all that stuff bottled up inside for so long, it needed to come out. It took a few seconds, and I could see he was struggling to find the right words to begin. I carefully placed our tiny glasses on the end table between us.

He glanced at it for a second, but instead of picking it up, he began, "My sergeant told me and a few other boys to go pick up the liquor for a party that was being given to sort of honor us soldiers. Apparently, the tide was turnin' and we were gainin' ground. Patton was even goin' to be there to give us a speech to tell us what a good job we were doin'. When you are in the middle of it, it don't look like much most of the time. Several battalions were comin' together for the celebration. We were to pick up a load of liquor to deliver to the banquet hall. I had not been feelin' well for a while. Hadn't held much down in the previous few days. I knew what was wrong with me, though," he said assuredly. "I figured it'd go away by itself pretty soon."

Now that sounded familiar. A man throwing up for days but still thinkin' he didn't need to go to a doctor. Of course, the thought immediately ran through my head that perhaps a doctor may not have been readily available at that point. I wondered about that for just a moment as I heard him say, "We had been marchin' into France, and sometimes supplies would run out, and we'd be without food for days. It was durin' one of those times, when we'd been without any food for a while and was starvin' plum to death. We came up on another troop that fed us. I knew when we were eatin' it, it had gone bad. We were so hungry we wolfed it down anyway, and a bunch of us got real sick. Most of the fellers had got over it, but for some reason, I couldn't seem to shake it." His eyebrow furrowed a bit as if questioning that still.

"Anyway," he picked back up, "we went and picked up the load, and on the way to the banquet hall, we ran into the awfullest traffic I'd ever seen. It was a complete standstill for some reason, and we couldn't get around it. I was worried we were never gonna get there. Then I spotted an alleyway that would shoot us across, avoiding the traffic and gettin' us to the hall on time…probably." He raised his head and grinned.

I looked at him seriously. "Please tell me it wasn't one of your famous shortcuts," I said this, very concerned since I had experienced Daddy's short-cuts a few times before. He was famous for them, actually. They usually took twice as long and could often get a little treacherous. What instantly came to mind was when we were on a ride to a place called Big Rock. We headed out early one morning on our horses and a few wagons. We only took something for lunch since it was supposed to be a short ride, and we should have been back long before dinner, certainly long before dark.

Then Daddy suggested we take a shortcut. My sisters and I exchanged worried glances. Nobody said a word, though. We just followed right along. Then lo and behold, we came upon another split in the path. I could tell he was a little unsure of which way to go. However, Daddy put on that "I know exactly where we are" face and assured everyone we were on the right track and not far from home.

We continued on and on and on. A few hours went by. Then it started drizzling rain and getting a bit cool. Not to mention, lunch had been light. I think we had a can or two of sardines to share with some crackers. When packing up, we had thought that was sufficient; it would be just a short ride.

Yep. Now, don't get me wrong. His shortcuts did not just pertain to rides through the woods on horseback. Oh, no, you might be driving to the next town over, and he'd find a shortcut that would turn it into an all-day road trip instead of just a boring thirty minutes or so. Honestly, we loved every second of it. On this particular ride, though, our short jaunt had turned into a much longer one. My niece Summer was very young, maybe eight or nine at the time, and she was starting to get hungry. She would ask repeatedly, "Are we almost there, Grandpa?"

He kept saying it was just a little ways yet and we'd be there soon. Then she started saying, "Grandpa, I'm hungry." To which he replied, "There's a McDonald's just right around that next turn up there." Of course, we were in the middle of the woods, not near any kind of civilization. Summer, however, got very excited and said, "Oh, good!" Then we got around that curve, and nothing, nothing except for trees. She'd ask again, "Where is it, Grandpa?" To which he would reply, jetting his chin forward assuredly, "It's just right up yonder."

Amazingly, she kept lookin' for it. That elusive McDonald's in the middle of the woods where there were no roads, no structures of any sort. Then it started really raining, and we were cold and hungry. My sisters and I kept giving each other worried glances because it was also startin' to get dark. We had no lanterns and were very ill-equipped for a night in the woods, which tended to get *very* dark very fast.

I used to sleep in the woods on the ground all the time, never thought twice about it, with nothing but a sleeping bag and some junk food. I'm just not as tough as I used to be. I cannot even begin to explain our delight when we finally came out into a familiar clearing, a recognizable field near our homeplace.

Yayyyyyy! my inside voice squealed in delight. I looked over and spotted a look of relief on Daddy's face too. He caught my eye and grinned. Then as calm as ever, he said, "See, I told ya we weren't lost." Yeah, right. I laughed out loud when I heard little Summer's voice say seriously, "I thought we were goin' to McDonald's?" Bless her little heart.

I was still smiling from the remnants of one of the coldest, warm memories I ever had when Daddy brought me back to the story at hand as he continued, "I spotted a one-way street. It was narrow. Only one vehicle could fit through, and we'd be goin' the wrong way."

He made a face that clearly said, on hindsight, he might ought to have taken all that into more of a serious consideration. "Of course," I said, smiling.

Smiling also, he explained, "Roscoe and the other fellows didn't think we should try it, but I said, 'Oh, it'll be all right, and we're never gonna make it if we don't.' So we turned down the narrow one-lane alleyway and headed on. It looked clear at first, and I was feelin' pretty good about it until we got almost to the end." He stopped and took a small sip from the little glass between us. I looked at mine but had not quite worked up the courage yet.

Then he continued, "All of a sudden, I spotted a convoy headed straight for us. My heart dropped. I figured I'd got us all in a whole bunch of trouble. We pulled to a stop, and I told all the fellers I'd handle it. Just stay in the vehicle. I knew I'd have to take the blame for this'n'. I got out and immediately stood to attention in front of a master sergeant that had exited the vehicle directly in front of us. He yelled, real gruff-like, 'Son, what *are* you doin'?' He didn't sound none too happy."

Daddy explained with a shake of his head. However, I could see a slight grin hiding behind his eyes, so I knew it must not have gone too wrong. Then he chuckled just a little and explained, "I stammered a bit, tryin' to come up with an answer that might suit him, and just said, 'I'm sorry, sir. We're tryin' to get this load of liquor to the banquet tonight. We was havin' trouble getting through the traffic and—'

"He put his hand up and cut me off midsentence and began to yell at me." Daddy was fightin' a grin as he recalled the incident. "He was still soundin' right unhappy as he said, 'So you thought you could just defy all the laws and come speedin' through this narrow—'"

Then Daddy turned to me with a serious look and said, "I wanted to correct him. We weren't speedin', but then all of a sudden, he stopped yellin' and turned around as we both heard another car door slam shut. I couldn't see who had gotten out of the vehicle 'til he got right up to us. When I saw that man's face, my heart stopped. I just knew I done got us all in a heap of trouble." Daddy now lowered his head, shaking it back and forth slightly. "Standin' there, starin' me down, was General Patton himself," he said, raising his head back up. "I stood at attention, holdin' my breath, waitin' for it…

"The sergeant that had gotten out first and had been yelling at me just stood there real quiet too. Then General Patton looked at me, eye to eye, we was, and never movin' his focus, he yelled real loud-like, "Men, we need to move out of these boys' way. They have got work to do." All of a sudden, the sergeant was jumpin' back into his vehicle without another word. General Patton stood there for a second and then said, "Son, it's fellows like you that is getting the job done here. Your country owes you a great debt for your service. Now, I want you to listen to me,' he said, lowering his voice just a little. 'As soon as you get this delivery done and the banquet is over, I want you to report to the infirmary. You understand?' He gave me a real serious stare.

"I must have looked a little confused, 'cause that was not what I expected to hear. I just stood there mouth hangin' open, I reckon, starin' right back... at General Patton," he reiterated. "I still hadn't quite comprehended what he'd said when he yelled a little louder. 'You understand? Infirmary. Before the banquet if you want, but definitely *straight* after.' He repeated his orders and made sure I understood. Then he just turned and got back in the vehicle. The whole convoy started backing all the way out of that narrow roadway the way they came in."

I could tell by the faraway look in Daddy's eyes, it was as if he was right back there again, standing in front of the famous general, slightly awed, it seemed. We both, then, took a short breath and sipped carefully from our tiny glasses. I was surprised at how the moonshine tasted exactly like the ripest, freshest peach I'd ever had. The difference was the trail of warmth that flowed smoothly down my throat and into my tummy. I smiled up at him, and he gave me back that sly grin of his.

"Told ya it was good," he said.

I was, as he would put it, right surprised.

CHAPTER 6

The Escape

"I *did* go to the infirmary, just like the general ordered, right after the banquet," he began. "Then they put me in the hospital." He huffed in a manner I recognized as annoyance and began telling me about his great escape from a hospital in France. "As it turned out, I had hepatitis. We had wallowed in a lot of unsanitary conditions, and hepatitis was not uncommon. I knew I'd been feelin' pretty rough," he said with a frown.

"The bad part was that we, my whole troop, that is, was scheduled to ship out to go home in just a few days. I wanted to go home so bad I couldn't stand it. They told us we would be home for Christmas.

Some would be done and get to stay, others were not quite finished yet. In those days, it went on a point system, and I was just a few points shy of bein' finished. Plans were, I could go home for a few weeks' leave, and then I would have to go to the Pacific side. I was really dreadin' that. I'd heard it was really bad over there."

"But you never made it to the Pacific, right?" I asked.

"No," he said, shakin' his head. "I got put in the hospital and separated from the rest of my troop. I tried every way I could to get out of it, but the doctor insisted I be admitted immediately. I wanted to talk to my buddies and make sure somebody would take care of Schnapps."

"Who was Schnapps?" I asked.

"Aw, he was the little puppy I had picked up," he said as if that was normal.

"Puppy?" I said questioningly. "Really, Daddy, you were in a foreign land, fightin' a war, you had hepatitis, and you were worried about a puppy?" After I said this out loud, it occurred to me that would be normal for him.

He went on to explain where the puppy came in. "We were goin' through a French village that the Germans had all but destroyed. Most of the homes were barely standin', if standin' at all. We were searchin' through the rubble for survivors. That was what we did, ya know," he said, shaking his head a bit. He took a short breath. "Anyway, this little beagle came runnin' out from under some rubble. I reached down and picked up the poor little fellow. He was half-starved and shakin' all over. I figured he was probably in shock."

Ahhh, of course. A beagle. Daddy always had a soft spot for beagles.

"We fed him. All the boys shared their food with the little fellow. He kind of became our mascot." Then he continued, "I knew the boys would take care of him," then he paused again, seemingly worried as he said, "as best they could.

"I tried to talk the doctors into lettin' me go a few more times, but they wouldn't hear of it. They had all my papers locked away where I couldn't get to 'em." I saw it rise again, plain as day. That Tabor stubborn that would not ever take no for an answer. It was a look I had seen many times over the years. Then he said, "I was lookin' for a way to sneak out but couldn't figure out how I'd be able to catch up to my troop. Walkin', I wouldn't get far, for sure. Where I was would've been about one hundred miles or so from the pier where they were due to ship out."

Then I caught that grin again, just slightly. "Then a chaplain came to visit." At that point, that grin had spread all the way to his eyes and told me very plainly he'd devised a plan.

"Poor fellow," I whispered just under my breath. I knew that chaplain didn't stand a chance. "So how did you make your escape? How did you get your papers?" I asked all at once.

"It wasn't easy, but I convinced him that I was healthy enough to make it. Getting home was my main goal at that point, even if it was only for a few short weeks. I could go to a doctor once I got there, I figured. All I needed was a ride. He said he had to make his rounds and would need to leave in about thirty minutes. He promised if I could make it out to the parkin' lot, he'd take me to the pier. If I wasn't there when he got ready to leave, he'd go on without me. I don't think he thought I'd make it out and he'd be off the hook."

He looked at me with that sly grin again as he repeated the conversation. "I told him 'That's fair enough. I'll see ya in about thirty minutes.'"

His determination is hard to describe, really. I swear it could literally move mountains or just make them crumble. Not out of fear. It's more of an unbending, unmoving, indescribable, unwavering belief that there is no, no, *no* such thing as you can't. He grinned again and said, "Well, I was afraid to try and change clothes in my room. I knew I'd be caught, for sure. So I got my uniform out of the drawer. The hospital had washed and folded it up real neat-like. I wrapped myself up in a blanket and tucked it underneath. Made like I was just walking down the hall to the bathroom. I remember one of the nurses lookin' up and saying in her thick accent, 'Mar…shall, do you need help to the *salle de bains*, my dear?'"

I laughed as he tried to mock her French accent, which still came out deeply southern.

He went on, "I shook my head and said, 'Naw, I can make it just fine. Thank ya.' I was weak and tryin' hard to sound convincin'. She gave me a look like she wasn't so sure. I was afraid she was goin' to insist. So I turned away and scurried on past her as quick as I could. Out the corner of my eye, I saw her give a grunt, put her head down, and go back to what she was doin'. I breathed a real sigh of relief and ducked into the bathroom door."

"So what happened?" I asked, wide-eyed. It's weird. I knew how this story ended. At least, I knew he must have made it out. Yet somehow, here I was, on the edge of my seat, holding my breath.

Then he went on, "I got into the bathroom and changed clothes. After I was done, I poked my head out, real slow-like. I listened for voices and footsteps. When the coast was clear, I straightened up and tried not to look like a patient. If I didn't see any of the nurses or doctors that knew me, they'd think I was a visitor. I headed toward the nearest exit. At one point, I heard some nurses comin' down the hallway around the corner, and I jumped into a janitor's closet. After they passed by, I just crept out slow and walked right out."

He raised his chin in the air and seemed very satisfied with himself just then. "When I went out to the parkin' lot, I wasn't sure which car was his, so

I stayed hid around a corner until I saw him walkin' out. He was right surprised to see me." He was chuckling too as he recalled the look on that poor fellow's face. Then he said, "I noticed he looked a little worried and maybe was havin' second thoughts. So I said, 'Now, sir, a man of the cloth must keep his promises, right?' He started out like he might try and argue but then just shrugged his shoulders and opened the car door. Defeatedly, he said, 'Get in.'

"We headed out toward Le Harvre. It would take a few hours to get there, so we had plenty of time to get to know each other a bit. First thing he wanted to know was why I was in such a hurry to get out of that hospital and couldn't wait 'til I was better. I explained that I only had a little time to work with and pretty soon would have to go to the South Pacific. I didn't really know if the Army would give me any extra time or not for bein' sick. If they were short men, I doubted it. I sure did not want to spend what little time I had in a hospital in France. I told him about Ruby, my family. I remember thinkin' he sure did ask a lot of questions. I figured he had a right to know what he had gotten himself into, so I might as well answer 'em."

Pausing again to gather his memories, he took a bite out of a Little Debbie cake. I followed suit.

"I filled him in on where I was from. I told him all about my big family, about Ruby. I told him all about Hershel, how he'd gone in ahead of me and I'd lied about my age, tryin' to catch up to him and then learned he'd gotten hurt and been sent home."

We sat in silence for just a second as I tried to imagine the conversation between Daddy and this total stranger, someone he would never likely see again. I caught a slight forlorn expression on his face as the memories were scattering about in his head.

Then he quickly straightened and said, "When we got close to the pier, sure enough, there was thousands of GIs tryin' to get on two ships. Then I remembered I didn't have my papers. I knew that could be a real problem. The chaplain noticed the look on my face and asked what was wrong. I told him that I had not been able to get to my papers. All my ID and everything was locked up back at that hospital. He gave me a worried look back and said, 'Go line up. I'll see what I can do.' We got out of the car and walked up to the Red Cross representative who was there helping with the sorting out who was who and what line they were supposed to get in."

Then Daddy straightened slightly and turned to look at me with that grin spreading wide and said, "Then I heard a dog barkin'. I looked out to see Schnapps runnin' right at me. I bent down and grabbed him, and oh Lord," he said, "I was never so proud to see anything in my life as I was to see that little fella. He was lickin' my face and, thank goodness, wasn't showin' any signs of that shell-shocked, starving little puppy he'd been when I first found him. You gotta understand," he paused to look me in the eye seriously, "we'd been through a whole lot together. Through many a battle, hunkered together in foxholes, he'd stick right to me. Then side by side, marchin' all the way across France."

He took a sudden breath and said, "Then I heard another familiar voice. It was Roscoe. He was headin' my way with a big smile on his face and yelled, 'Marshall! I was afraid we'd lost you!' Big, burly Roscoe then gave me a hug. I was glad to see him too. The other boys came up, and we were all tickled to be together again, excited about goin' home for a bit. We got to catch up for a few minutes, and then I turned to see the chaplain talkin' to the Red Cross rep as he was pointin' my way. I kept my fingers crossed he was havin' some luck. I was not sure what exactly he'd be able to do, but if he could get me on that ship home, I'd sure 'nuff be grateful."

Hanging his head, he shook it slightly as he said, "I watched both of them talking seriously. I tried to make out what they were sayin' but couldn't really figure out which way the conversation was goin'. After a bit, the chaplain turned toward me and started walking my way. I couldn't read his expression at first, but as he came closer, I saw him start to smile." With a huff, Daddy said, "I knew then I was goin' home."

Repeating the conversation from so long ago, he said, "'Marshall, I explained to them about your *missing* papers.' He gave me a look that let me know not to mention anything about where mine actually were. 'You are good to go, son. Go home to that red-head of yours.'"

I knew then that Daddy had talked to him more about Momma than he had let on. I smiled.

Then he said, "I wasn't sure what the chaplain had told them, but I didn't care so long as I was getting on a ship headin' west! We were all real excited boardin'. Most of us had not seen US soil in two or more years. Spirits were real high. Of course, the fellers goin' home for good were the most excited. But at that point, I just had my mind on goin' home. No need to worry beyond that just yet. We all agreed that once we got the chance, we'd never leave US soil again."

That would certainly explain why Daddy was never much of a traveler. Momma, on the other hand, was ready to go before she knew what the destination was. Just like me. Daddy had made up his mind to go home, and using his famous Tabor determination, it looked like he had succeeded. Maybe. This story was not over yet.

"They were separating us, puttin' some on one ship and some on the other," he started again. "I was glad Roscoe and I were in the same group. Just as it looked like we were all headin' home, one of the men in charge came over to me and said, 'Son, I'm afraid you can't take that dog on the ship with you.'

My heart dropped. I heard all the guys around sayin', 'Oh, come on. You gotta let him take Schnapps! He's carried him all through this war!' But they wouldn't give in, and eventually, it came down to Schnapps was not allowed to leave his country. Period. I asked the Red Cross rep if he would promise to make sure my dog got a good home and was taken care of. He reached out and took him from me. He looked at Schnapps and then back at me and said, 'I promise. I'll make sure he gets a good home.'"

Daddy took a breath and looked at me then. "It was the best I could do. This was the second time I had had to do this exact same thing. Just let go and hope for the best."

He hung his head as the slightest hint of a tear came into the corner of his big brown eyes. We were both holdin' our breath in hopes little Schnapps had had a good life. It suddenly occurred to me at that moment, there's not a thing wrong with a little moonshine.

*****

It was time for a break, an *Andy Griffith* break to be exact. I think we both needed a little distraction. Mom sat with us, and we watched a lighthearted episode featuring the Darlings. It was one of my favorites. We laughed as we watched the one where the Darling family was trying to make Andy commit Opie's hand in marriage to the newborn Darling baby. At that point, Opie was maybe ten. I looked over at Daddy and Momma laughing and thought, *What an awesome sight.*

I had decided to stay there that night. I planned to sleep on the couch. Daddy had gotten to where he was up and down a lot at night. He didn't sleep well. I was afraid if I was back in one of the bedrooms, I wouldn't hear if he woke up and maybe needed someone to talk too. It's funny how precious time gets when you can see it slipping away.

My eyelids began to get heavy, and I could feel my body giving in to a relaxed and dreamy state when, suddenly, a thought scurried through my head like a tiny little mouse.

"*Second* time I had to let go and hope for the best," I heard his sweet voice say.

*****

We had all been asleep for a while when I heard a stirring in the kitchen, a rattling of paper I recognized immediately as Little Debbie wrappers. I raised up and headed into the kitchen. I walked in as he was pouring a glass of milk.

"Can't sleep?" I asked.

"Oh, I sleep in short increments these days, a little here and a little there," he explained. He held up the box of Little Debbie cakes and said, "Want one?"

My head said no, but my heart said yes, or was it my taste buds? Either way, I gave in, as usual. I poured myself a glass of milk. We then took a stool at the island and began munching, silently at first.

Then he said, "I was thinkin' about the ship. To this day, I can't figure out how we didn't sink." He had that distant look in his eyes again, like he was right back there. He started, "I'd heard storms could be really bad in the North Atlantic, but I never imagined they'd be anything like what I saw though." He took a small bite of a chocolate cake filled with white cream.

Then he began telling me another story, "Christine wrote letters to me all the time. I guess like you did Larry when he was in Vietnam. You have no idea how important it is to get letters from home when you are overseas like that."

He stopped to munch a little more on his tasty cake before adding, "I got a letter from Christine that said your grandma woke your grandpa up in the middle of the night and told him either I or Hershel had just been dropped off at the bus station and was home on leave. He thought she had been dreamin' and tried to get her to go back to bed, but she insisted that he get up and take them to the bus station. He did, and when they were just about at the station, they saw Hershel walking toward them on the side of the road. Hershel was shocked to see 'em and asked how they knew he was there. Your grandpa just said,

'Your Momma seems to know everything when it comes to you boys.'"

After a short pause, he said, "Your grandma sure had a sixth sense about things." With that, he said, "I think I'll go lay back down fer a bit."

I nodded my head and said, "Okay." Then I looked at him and kissed the top of his forehead and said, "I love you so much, Daddy." I felt a great heaviness in light of all I had learned. He looked at me and blessed me once more with that grin as he turned toward the hall. I watched as he made his way back to his room. I remembered all the times we had danced up and down that hallway and then out to the living room and 'round the wall that separated the front room from the kitchen and dining area, all the way around and back again. I could see him and Mom laughing and twirling. I could hear the music, the voices, all those beautiful voices. "Do-si-do and round we go." I could almost taste Mom's popcorn balls, made, of course, with sorghum made by the local Mennonites. Maybe that is what made them so special. I have never found any since that compared.

Gathering here on snow days was the best. When we got tired of dancing, we'd play cards and board games. One Thanksgiving Day, my sisters and I jumped on top of Mom's slate top coffee table and belted out the entire *Young Turks* album by Rod Stewart. Yep, we were adults. By the end of the day, I believe we had worn that album out. Thank goodness Mom knew to buy sturdy furniture. Many years later, Mom talked about that, smiling, saying it was one of her favorite memories. I remember when, in lieu of a dining room table, Mom actually purchased a plexiglass dance floor instead. I wondered briefly where she had found that and what had happened to it. Did we wear it out as well? Perhaps.

Then I caught sight of a vision of Daddy hanging onto that half-sunk ship, sick, freezing. How close we came to never existing and never having any of those moments. How does one thank God for his gift of life? For saving that man I have been so lucky to call Daddy. He might have only been 5'7", but I have always seen him as ten feet tall. What words could ever say how blessed we've been?

I fell asleep eventually but could never quite answer that question.

CHAPTER 7

Our Twisty, Turny Paths

"Good morning," I said as I met Mom at the coffee pot.

"Good morning," she said. I noticed something different in her voice.

"Did you sleep okay?" I asked, concerned.

"Ummmm, not really. I guess I fell asleep listening to you and your dad talking last night." She paused as if in thought. "I remember when we were planning to be married. I was a little nervous about it all. Confused even." She looked up at me with an odd expression.

"Confused?" I asked. We settled on the barstools at the counter, sipping our coffee.

She lowered her head a bit and said, "At first, I was not so sure marriage and children was in the cards for me. When I agreed to marrying your dad, it still seemed so *distant*. I remember the point at which the truth of it was sinking in. I would be getting married soon. I prayed every night that the war would end and Marshall would make it back. Then I prayed I would still be here and able to be a wife and mother. That word sunk like a stone. I wondered if I would be able to do that. The latest doctor had said I would never survive childbirth. Of course, the doctor before him had said I would never live to be an adult."

I had never fully understood the weight she had carried her whole life, living with such a threat within her own body that no one had an answer for.

"I have a mind to think that doctors don't know that much," she said emphatically.

"I cannot even imagine…" I said softly.

"I was sitting at my sewing machine one day, making a special skirt suit, my wedding suit, thinking, obviously, I had made it to adulthood," she said in a "So there" kind of way.

I grinned and asked, "What did it look like?"

"It was made of winter-white wool, fully lined with rayon. It had seams from the busts to the waist and a scalloped hem along the edge of the jacket that sat at the waist. It was double-breasted with six mother-of-pearl buttons. Momma actually gave me those off an old suit of hers she had grown out of."

She got a quizzical look on her face and said, "I had not noticed Momma gaining any weight, but that was the excuse she gave me anyway." She smiled. "I didn't argue. It felt good to be carrying something of her with me. That would be my something old, she had said. The skirt fit around the hips with a flared hem. I needed something blue, so I found a light-baby-blue trim to add to the edges of the collar and hem. I made a small pillbox hat to match from the leftover material. I used a small piece of silky blue material to fashion a rose and add just enough netting for a veil that came to right below my eyes, to the edge of my cheekbones."

She was moving her hands to show where the veil lay.

"Suddenly, I heard a knock at the front door. When I opened it, to my surprise, there stood Mr. and Ms. Tabor. I wondered for just a moment if the front porch was able to hold her. She was no small woman." We both chuckled a little. Momma always said just what she thought.

"Ms. Tabor had her hair pulled back in a bun. It was gray then, but at one time had been black as coal. She was dark skinned. The opposite of Mr. Tabor. He was white as a sheet and barely weighed enough not to blow away. They both had those big brown eyes. Marshall was a good mix of the two. Built more like

Mr. Tabor but had his mother's black hair and dark skin. Some say she was at least part Cherokee. From her looks, I would guess they might be right.

"Thing is, I was always happy to see them, but surprised. They usually didn't come by during the week. She had become like another mother to me." I could feel the warmth in her voice as she spoke of my late grandmother.

"Mr. Tabor was a very quiet man, except at church. I had wondered what on earth got into him when he stood before a pulpit. He was mostly mild-mannered, and yet put a pulpit in front of him and he could suddenly jump three feet in the air while excitedly exclaiming the Lord's mercy. There was no wonder why he stayed so skinny." We both laughed.

"I was taking their coats and offering them coffee when Mom and Dad came in to greet them. I laid their coats on top of my bed and went to the kitchen to start a pot of coffee. I could hear their conversation, and as usual, it turned to war news very quickly. It was hard to think of anything else most times. It consumed the days and your dreams at night. Everyone had someone—a brother, a son, a husband—to worry about. Everyone had different news to share. Letters from loved ones, rumors they had heard. Word traveled fast even without cell phones, actually, without any phones. Although the letters were often vague and secretive, there were often hints to decipher. Everyone was glued to their radios in the evenings, of course."

She had a sadness in her tone, remembering. "I was busy in the kitchen when I heard their conversation. Mr. Tabor was speaking in a low voice of what he had heard most recently. Families were being rounded up and taken to camps by the train car and busloads. Even children, women, elderly. It didn't sound real. Why would Hitler want to capture his own people? I heard the words 'Aryan race,' 'a historic, higher mission,' Hitler had said. As Mr. Tabor repeated these confusing and ominous-sounding words, even though I couldn't quite comprehend them, I felt a sense of evil that was far too much to accept. Suddenly, I heard footsteps behind me and turned quickly to see Ms. Tabor coming into the kitchen. 'My dear, I have something I could use your help with,' she said.

"'Of course. What can I do?' I had no doubt that whatever she asked of me, I would most certainly be happy to do it. 'My girls, well, they grow so fast, and the thing is, I'm having a hard time keeping up. I've seen your work. You have a real talent for sewin'. Since the boys have gone, there's not been a lot to smile about. I was hopin' you'd help me make the girls a nice dress for winter. I know it's not much, but I think it could lighten their spirits a bit—in the meantime, keep their behinds covered. Those girls are all long legs, ya know! I swear they grow an inch every time I turn around. So do you have time? I know you don't go to school anymore. I thought maybe—'

"'I would love to!' I answered. 'I even have some material we can use and several patterns to choose from.' This actually sounded like fun. Other than music, sewing was my next favorite thing to do. It occurred to me, almost instantaneously, Ms. Tabor had never had trouble clothing her family before, and I really doubted Hershel and Marshall helped much in that department. I smiled at the thought. It was as if I was being folded right into the family.

"With her mission accomplished, she went back in to the conversation with Mom and Dad and Mr. Tabor. I served the coffee, picking up most of what they were saying but half refusing to accept it. I began to imagine myself part of that big, bustling, busy bunch of Tabors, Ruby Jewell Tabor, or would I drop the Jewell and just be Ruby Kerley Tabor? I had to smile. Any way you put it, I would be Mrs. Marshall Tabor. It had a real nice ring to it. But then I noticed something else stirring deep inside that somewhat faulty heart of mine, something I could not quite put my finger on. Marshall was the most handsome man for miles around. A good man. Even Dad thought so. All the girls were jealous that he had actually picked me. I was a little surprised myself. I remember the first time I saw him. I had gone with Dad to their house. He had to see Mr. Tabor about something. Walking into their house, the first thing that caught my eye, of course, was all the piles of shoes at the door. Then I looked up and met directly in the eye, Marshall Tabor. He was maybe fourteen years old. He was just staring at me as if I had a big bug on my forehead. I noticed a solemn, almost sad look in his eyes. He didn't smile. Didn't say a word. Just looked at me intently for a few seconds. 'So serious,' I remember thinking. Then he turned and walked away." She sounded almost dreamy.

"So what was the something, Mom?" I asked.

She startled out of her thoughts and just simply said, "Fear."

I gave her an inquisitive look, prompting her to elaborate.

"Fear I would not live to see him come back, fear of disappointing him and myself if I was not able to have kids. Fear that maybe getting married was not even what I wanted to do. Fear of being a burden, unable to take care of myself if—"

She sipped her coffee as she returned to her story, leaving me to imagine the ifs that had bombarded her throughout her life.

"I was excited to get started on making dresses for all the girls. That would be fun and take my mind off all the things there was to worry about," she began. "I had several patterns to show them all. I could even make patterns or alter them if they wanted. The older girls would help with the sewing, and we would all work together. When I arrived at the Tabor home, they were all excited and ready to pick patterns and materials. We gathered all we had and laid it out on the table. Christine was a full-grown woman and had the shapely figure to prove it. At sixteen years of age, she was a true beauty. She picked a solid color of red for her new dress. It would be perfect for her coloring. I suggested we add a matching cloak to go with it and was delighted to see her eyes light up. Willene, fifteen and still in the process of filling out, skinny and cute as a button, chose a blue-and-whited-checkered-patterned material and, of course, wanted a cloak just like her big sister. I recommended we go with a matching solid blue for the cloak, and she too was delighted. I thought at that moment what a wise woman Ms. Tabor was. She not only understood the importance of the physical challenges to raising a family but she understood how to give them hope—hope, every bit as important as food, clothing, or shelter. I remember making a mental note of that." She looked at me pointedly.

"The girls were all smiles, picking out their favorite styles and exchanging ideas of trim, ribbons. It was fun just watching them," she said, smiling.

"One by one, we measured hips, busts, and those long Tabor legs while chatting away. Then we realized we may have gotten a little loud because we apparently woke up baby Jo from her nap. Her name is actually Jo, middle name Ann. Marshall named her after his horse, of course. I remember asking Ms. Tabor, 'What about baby Jo? She should have something new as well, don't you think?' She replied,

'Well, she hardly'll notice. I didn't want to overload ourselves.' I said, 'No problem. I don't have any baby patterns, but I can make one, and she needs to be included. Besides, I haven't had an opportunity to make baby clothes before. I should probably learn.' But when those words came out, there was a sharp, unwanted, unwelcome feeling in the pit of my stomach. Your Grandma Tabor sensed it and told me not to worry. She said everything was going to work out just fine as she patted my hand."

Mom reached over and imitated Grandma patting my hand. She had a forlorn expression as she said, "It was almost like she knew. I had worried that maybe I was actually still cursed somehow. Mom never really explained it, but that curse put on me as an infant had something about firstborn muttered in it. Not that I would take such things so seriously, and yet…" Her voice trailed off.

I thought of Tony, firstborn, surely not. I quickly pushed that thought away.

She seemed a bit forlorn as she explained, "Thing is, a doctor later told Mom and Dad that squalling like I did may have saved my life. He said it had made my heart stronger. If I had just slept, like most babies, I probably would not have awakened."

We all, especially as children, have fears and bad dreams. Knowing we are healthy, we often fear death. How would it feel to know each night when she closed her eyes there was a very good chance she would not be able to open them the next morning? That her heart could really just stop at any moment? Hearing doctors' amazement that it hadn't happened already each time a stethoscope was put up to her chest? My heart broke for her.

"I also still had those dreams stirring to be like Patsy Cline, Peggy Lee," I heard her say. "The life they must have had. Traveling all over the place, singing, and playing their music. Seeing one exciting city after another. How glamorous," she said, smiling dreamily.

With new eyes, I looked upon this woman I had never truly seen. "I love you, Mom."

CHAPTER 8

Wedding Bells and Other Scary Stories

"One Sunday we were all up early getting ready for church. We always wore our Sunday best," Mom said.

"I had on a purple A-line dress with a small Peter Pan collar made of polyester lined with rayon. It had long sleeves and black faux-fur trim around the wrist. Handmade, of course. Since that first snow, that night I was out with Ole Joe, it had really started turning cold." She got a distant look in her eyes.

"Secretly, I thought to myself, that's good. Marshall will be back soon," she said matter-of-factly. Then she continued, "I remember the butter-flies filling my stomach at that thought. My wedding suit was hanging up and ready for wear. In just two weeks, he would actually be returning, and we would be officially married."

We both took a sip from our wineglasses we had gotten prior to sitting down to do another walk down memory lane.

"We had decided to just elope. If we crossed the state line into Georgia, we wouldn't have to get the blood test and wait three days before we could get married like you had to in Tennessee. In Georgia, you could just walk right into the courthouse, get your license, and get married the same day, which was much quicker and simpler since we only had a short amount of time to work with. I had been busy going through my clothes and belongings to weed out what I could and couldn't pack to take with me. I was really nervous about leaving Dad with Mom. He kept assuring me he could handle things. Wintertime was a slow time, he kept telling me. What he didn't say, but we all knew, was I would be back very soon. Marshall would be shipping out.

"Marshall and I decided that I would come back to live with Mom and Dad while he was overseas. Our time together would be short. We knew that from the start. He would ship out, and then the real worries would begin."

She took a deep breath and slowly sipped her wine again. "I decided" she said sternly, "I would not worry while he was still here. It wouldn't do any good anyway. Worryin' never changed a thing. Your wedding day should be a happy day. I determined it would not be clouded by all the uncertainties. We would just enjoy whatever moments we would be given…up until the last."

She continued, "Anyway, we went to church, and after a somewhat interesting service, we were all headed over to the Tabors' house. I say interesting because, honestly, I never understood half what the preacher was saying. It wasn't Mr. Tabor that time. In that service, he sat quietly in the pews with only an 'Amen' and nod of the head every now and then. What I didn't understand was, why shout all the time? And that pounding on the pulpit…really?"

She shook her head and smiled. "Seemed more like they were just puttin' on a show as far as I could tell. If you had two services, it became almost a contest of who had the spirit the most. I remember Dad looking over at me, wishing I would change the expression of whatever it was on my face. I didn't necessarily feel I had control over that. I did try, though. I didn't laugh out loud. That was an accomplishment!" She laughed out loud as she said it.

"We walked from the church house to the Tabors' house. It wasn't very far. Those who lived further away, like us, had driven to the church from home. We would leave our cars in the parking lot and walk together. I remember James coming up and walking beside me. He looked up at me with his big Tabor brown eyes and said pointedly, 'So I hear you are going to be my sister soon.' It wasn't really a question, more of a statement."

"He was perhaps twelve or so, I think, at the time, so I explained that yes, I was planning on it, very soon, in fact, I said with a smile. There was a slight little niggle again. It was a cross between being excited and maybe a dread of some sort. I heard those whispers again unwelcomingly going through my brain: 'She'll never live to be an adult…or even if she does, she will never survive childbirth.' Then I thought of Ms. Tabor's *knowing* assurance. I hoped she was right.

"My thoughts were interrupted by James's voice saying, 'I guess that'll be okay. I mean, I like you, like a sister 'n' all.' He was cute when he said it. I think I may have sensed a bit of jealousy there. Maybe a slight crush? Every time Marshall and I had been at the Tabors' house, James always sat close to me. Flirted in that little boy way. 'I think you'll make a great little brother,' I told him. Then he let me know in no uncertain terms, he was almost all grown up, with Hershel and Marshall both gone, practically the man of the family, he said. He began to explain how he was in charge of taking care of Joe, milking the cows, and doing all of Hershel's and Marshall's chores around the farm. I smiled at the thought of Ole Joe. I did not want to remind James of this just then, but that part was not working out quite as intended. As a matter of fact, Joe was still in our barn from his last escape. Seemed happy enough there, and I think Dad was getting tired of walking him back. It amazed me once again that Ole Joe was so persistent. Maybe he really did know something the rest of us didn't."

I smiled just thinking about it.

She looked at me and asked, "What?"

I snickered out loud. "Oh, nothing. Just picturing you anxiously awaiting Daddy's return alongside a horse."

She obviously thought that was funny too. Then she continued, "While we were walking, baby Jo started getting fussy, so I asked Ms. Tabor if I could carry her for a while. We were a bit chilled by the time we got inside the house, so I went into the family room to sit in front of the fireplace. I took the rocking chair in front of the fire so I could rock her and get her and me warmed up. The rest of the adults gathered in the kitchen and dining room. Traditionally, when there was a big gathering, the adults would get their plates first and then the kids. I always thought that was backward. I couldn't stand the thought of a child waiting behind me for food.

Another mental note, it would not be so in my home. Kids first, always. The adults can wait. Little Margie came in and sat in the floor in front of the fire beside us. She had a little doll she was playing with. She showed it to me proudly. It was a Raggedy Ann. Everyone seemed genuinely happy to have me be a part of their family. Except for Chris, maybe. I felt a hesitance in her. She was very protective of her big brother, I knew. I understood that. They are very close. Always had been. He, Hershel, and Christine were babies almost all at once. Worked side by side most days. Not without their squabbles, of course."

She started laughing a little as she recalled, "Christine would often lock the boys out of the house because they were so dirty and muddy from being up at the barn. She'd say, 'You will not be messin' up my house!' Then she would shove bologna underneath the crack in the door for them to eat."

We both laughed thinking of gritty bologna.

"All the little ones had gathered in the living room around me and were warming themselves by the fire. I noticed Paul. He looked so skinny and pale and was shivering. I grabbed a nearby quilt and wrapped it around him. Most of the other little ones were already too busy to sit still for long. They were an energetic bunch! I think that's when I decided I wanted a house full of little ones too. I wanted to be surrounded by all that energy. I remember asking Paul if he wanted me to get him something to eat.

He was all for that. Good, I thought. Maybe I can fatten him up a bit. I went in and got his plate for him ahead of everybody."

I saw a more solemn look appear as she said, "Everyone was gathered, talking about the war again. It consumed all conversations. I didn't think I could stand listening. I decided, again, not to let it get to me for the next few weeks. I would be happy. Marshall was coming home. We would be getting married. So I went back to where the kids were."

I said, "That must have been hard. Staying hopeful and positive during such a time. The world as a whole had to have looked awfully bleak."

She nodded in agreement. "That's why I chose the company of the younger ones. They made it seem much more hopeful. I sat down in the floor and was playing with baby Jo. I recall her looking at me so sweetly and cooing softly. She raised her little baby hand to my face and slightly pinched my nose. I giggled at her, and she smiled. I thought to myself right then, I can see me doing this. I leaned down and breathed in her sweet baby scent and thought, again, I *can* do this. Then as if I had all the control in the world, I decided the first one would be a boy. He'd have Marshall's jet-black hair and dark skin. I hoped he'd inherit that grin too. Then correcting myself, I decided, yes, he would have that grin!"

We both laughed. We looked at each other, knowing that is exactly how it had worked out. Tony, their firstborn, had had daddy's dark skin, black hair, and that grin.

Then she went on to say, "That was when I made a firm decision to go forward with my life. I would not let fear dictate my decisions. I would get married and have a house full of kids just like the Tabors! Then for the first time probably in my life, I felt a warm glow at the thought of the future. I would be married in about two weeks. No niggle. No regrets. No fears."

"So," I stated, "you and Aunt Christine seem close now. I guess I had thought you always had been. I never imagined it ever having been any different."

Then she explained, "Well, at that time, the talk was that I could wake up just about any time and be dead, I guess."

We laughed, and I said, "I'm really glad that didn't happen!"

"Plus," she went on, "I had always talked about going back to city life. I never was much of a country girl. She was afraid I wouldn't be happy staying here and being a farmer's wife. She was just afraid Marshall would end up hurt. Either I would leave, die, or be a burden on him if my health failed. It was understandable."

Mulling this over, I took another sip and asked, "What happened to your dreams, Momma?"

She looked at me and smiled. "They came true, don't ya know?" She smiled again. "Well, for the most part, I think. Maybe not living in a city, but I gave birth to my favorite audience, and there was never a shortage of music in this house!"

I looked around that house, that room. I remember it being built. Tony, Larry, Tim, Connie, Carolina, even me, Ronnie, and Jeff helped. I was maybe ten. Ronnie and Jeff, Tony's children, were six and four. We all pitched in. We little ones were gofers. We gathered stuff the adults needed such as nails, hammers, or other small items. We even helped lay shingles on the roof. Building the house was a family affair. Of course, living in it was even more so.

That house had always been so *full*. My guess is that Grandma and Grandpa Tabor's house must have been very much the same—gritty bologna, Daddy's pranks, and all.

CHAPTER 9

Letting Go, Once More

The sun showed up bright and early the next morning. I was not used to operating without my full eight hours of beauty sleep. I had slept well enough in that short amount of time. Only occasionally were my dreams haunted by the visions of my parents' past. Both were more daunting than I had ever imagined. Upon awakening, I noticed a heaviness in my heart that, for an instant, I couldn't quite place. Then I heard Daddy's voice in my head saying "the second time" he "had to let go and hope for the best." The story of Schnapps came to me in

bits and pieces as my eyelids begin their morning reg-
imen. One eye did the ol' 1-2-1-2, and then the other
eyelid, 1-2-1-2. I knew full well that was the closest I
would get to a workout that day.

I wondered, once more, what Daddy had meant
when he said "the second time I had to let go." I could
not wait to find out. We went through our routine
of breakfast, coffee, dishes, Granny, not necessarily
in that order.

When we settled down, I waited for the opportunity to jump back in. I was relieved to see he
had awakened in good spirits. I hoped he had not
dreamed of those terrible things we'd talked about
the night before. I wondered how often he had over
the years. He had, for as long as I remembered, been a
restless sleeper. We were used to him hollering out in
his sleep, even occasionally sleepwalking. It was not
always bad dreams, thankfully. Once he hollered out
his own name and got up to answer the door. Or he'd
call out a horse's name, and we knew he was loading
it, unloading it, training, or riding it. Momma woke
up to him lifting her leg up and down saying, "This
hinge is too long. We need to cut it off." Those were
the good dreams.

"Let's have a cup of coffee out on the patio.
Want to?" he asked, looking at me.

"Sure," I said, looking at Mom to see if she
was joining us. She was not always as excited to sit
out. She said bugs loved her too much. However, it

looked like she was up for an outside venture as well. We gathered our cups of coffee, all with cream, and headed for the front porch.

Momma and Daddy sat in the two-person swing, and I took a chair opposite them. I could not help but notice how cute they were sitting there together. I tried to imagine them young and in love. Then torn apart by war. I thought of a picture of them I had seen. It was taken the day he left. They were just kids. Their arms were wrapped tightly around each other with such solemn expressions. I can imagine he was wondering if her faulty heart would keep beating until he could get back. She was praying he would come back.

Again, my heart filled to its brim as I whispered a silent "Thank you, God." I took a deep breath and asked, "Daddy, last night you said something along the lines of you were having to let your puppy, Schnapps, go and hope for the best, and that was the second time you had had to do that."

Momma looked at Daddy and said, "Have you told her about the little boy yet?"

"No, I hadn't got to that one," he said.

I looked at him with a wrinkled brow and asked, "Little boy?"

"Yeah, well. Again, we were comin' into another village that had been all but destroyed. I spotted a house that was standin' a bit better than most and noticed a kid's bike laying in the front yard. We were splitting up to search it out. Figured I'd best start there. I had to move the broken front door out of the way and then proceeded real cautious-like. You never knew what might be waitin' inside. We had to watch for booby traps. Snipers were known to stay behind too, waitin' for us. I was movin' slow, tryin' to be quiet and listen for any sounds at al'. Once I got into the middle of what had been a living room, I heard a faint whimperin'. I crept closer, steppin' over broken wood, busted-up furniture, and shattered glass. Stayin' aware, focused, I stood real still and noticed a hand sticking up out of the rubble. Slowly, I moved as much debris off the body as I could. It was a woman, in her twenties, I guessed. I could tell by lookin' she wasn't alive, but I checked for a pulse anyway just to be sure. Carefully, I laid her arm back down and spotted another body beside hers. Man this time. I did the same for him, but he was gone too. The whole time I kept hearing that small whimper. I decided it was coming from a closet. I had a candy bar in my pocket, so I pulled it out and started talkin' real soft-like. 'You can come out now. I won't hurt ya none.' After a bit, I made my way across the room nearer to the sound. I didn't want to scare 'im any more than he had been already, so I hunkered down and kept repeatin' as I held up the candy bar, 'You can come out now. I have something for ya.'

"It took a few minutes before the door started slidin' back. Then a head poked out with dark curly hair. He was filthy dirty. His brown eyes were puffy and red. He was havin' a hard time pushin' the door back, so I moved closer and helped him. When he finally was able to step all the way out, I figured him to be about eight or nine. He probably hadn't had anything to eat in a few days. I couldn't tell for sure how far behind the Germans we were. I handed him the candy bar. He reached out slowly and took it, never takin' his eyes off me. I imagined he had probably been out ridin' that bike I saw. It would have started as just a low unfamiliar rumble, what with all those tanks, guns, and boots hittin' hard on the ground. Then the panic would've set in. I could almost see the whole thing play out, his parents hidin' him in the nearest place, covering him with coats or clothes. I looked at the distance between their bodies and the closet door, about eight feet."

He lowered his head, taking a breath. If I could have said anything, it might have been, "It's okay, you don't have to go into this." I didn't. I couldn't. All I could do was sit there, seemingly, sharing in a pain he had mostly carried alone. I felt so helpless.

"I held my hand out and told him I'd take care of 'im. Then I led him out of what had been his home just a few days before," he explained.

"What happened to him, Daddy?" I asked.

"He stayed close to me for a few days as we kept movin' toward Paris. My sergeant said we would try and find a Red Cross station or some safe place to leave him. Until then, we stuck close together. He didn't speak a lick of English, and I didn't speak French, but somehow, we understood each other just fine. We hid in foxholes at night. I noticed he was shakin' all over. It was warm, but he was still shiverin'. I'm sure he was in shock. I gave him my Army blanket and tried to reassure him I would do my best to take care of 'im."

He turned his head back to face me as he said, "We kept marchin' with only a few hours' sleep in between. He was a tough little feller. Never complained. I knew he had to be tired. His shoes were 'bout wore out, but he kept right up. It took about three or four days before we finally got to a small town. I's sure glad we found a safe place before we ran into any battles."

He shook his head and then explained, "We came to a small town that had not been hit. Best I could tell, he had relatives somewhere close by. It was early, and the sun was just startin' to rise. I took him and set him down on the sidewalk in front of a pharmacy. I tried to explain while pointin' to the store. 'Somebody will be here to open up soon. You wait right here, okay?' He nodded like he understood. I said, 'Let them know you need help and to take you to your family, ya hear?' There was tears running down his cheek, but he was trying to be strong. Then he threw his arms around my neck and squeezed tight. He was scared and shakin' all over. I held onto him for a minute and explained, 'I can't stay. I have to go now, but you're gonna be all right.' Then I heard the sergeant's voice behind me say, 'Marshall, we gotta go, and where we're going is gonna get real rough. This is the best you can do. You know it's not safe for him to be with us.'"

Daddy's voice shook. "I knew he was right. When I was headin' up the road with the rest of the men, I stopped just a little way off and looked back. I wanted to make sure he was waitin' there like I'd told him to. He was sittin' there just as I had left him, holdin' that old scratchy Army blanket. I knew I had to do whatever I could to make sure that war didn't get to him no more."

I saw that resolve. A sheer determination that was almost palatable. "I've wondered about him many a time over the years," he said with tear-filled eyes.

There was such a heaviness in the air. I looked over at Momma and Daddy and suddenly got one of my very brightest ideas if I have to say so myself. "Why don't we take a ride to Muddy Pond today?" I asked, instantly lightening our mood. They both straightened with a smile. A day trip sounded like an awesome idea. We all needed a break from all the rehashing we had been so intent on.

Muddy Pond is a Mennonite community situated between Crossville and a little town called Monterey. It is beautiful country. There is a general store that serves a great lunch and sells freshly baked breads, spices, fresh milk, and other farm-to-table goods. There is also another store that sells beautiful wood crafts, leather goods, and handmade furniture that the Mennonites are well-known for.

Daddy loved to go there, and Momma loved to go *anywhere*.

It turned out to be a beautiful, sunny day. As we arrived, we saw they had the mules hooked up to the turnstile, making sorghum. Daddy could watch those mules walk around in that circle for hours. Mom and I did a little shopping. We bought fresh spices, sourdough bread, and of course, sorghum. We had lunch at the little deli. Daddy took time to check out the bridals and saddles in the leather shop. He also had to look over the assortment of covered wagons, not that he needed another one of those, but to tell him so would be a little like telling me I did not need another pair of boots. Then after a while, we headed back home. We arrived just in time to see the bright reds, oranges, blues, and lavenders fill the sky as the sun sank behind the mountains. It was one of my favorite days.

That night, as I began to close my eyes, I imagined a drug store owner coming to open up his store. Upon seeing a child wrapped in a green Army blanket, sitting on the sidewalk directly in front of his door, he would bend down and say, "Can I help you, *petit garcon*?" After listening intently to the child's story, the store owner would lead him safely to his family, who then would embrace him and thank God he was safe and alive.

I wondered, does that child, man now, still hear Daddy's soft, comforting voice every now and then? Perhaps see the face of the young, American soldier when he closed his eyes? Does he wonder about that soldier as often as that soldier wonders about him? I *pray* that he has had a good life. Hopefully he is not haunted with nightmares but remembers the love and kindness of a stranger.

CHAPTER 10

Ruby Red and Uncle Paul

I crept quietly into the living room. Daddy was asleep in his big easy chair, and Mom was in her rocker, reading. I went over and kissed her cheek lightly. She looked up with a smile and laid her book down on the coffee table.

"Busy?" I asked.

"No, just reading a little while your daddy naps. Let's go in the kitchen," she said while getting up and heading that way. "We can talk and not wake him."

"Sounds good," I replied. I could tell she had something weighing on her mind. "What's up?" I asked.

"I was just thinking about when your dad was away." She took a moment, obviously dredging up a past that could seem so distant one minute yet had come rushing to the present very quickly. "I remember when that first dreadful winter finally ended. The warm breeze chasing away the winter chill felt unusually… *hopeful.*" A kind of clarity sparkled in her blue eyes.

"Winter always seems so dreary under ordinary circumstances," she began, "but with spring comes hope. Our soldiers were holding their own as best we could tell in those faraway lands on both sides of the world. Most of ours from this area were in Europe. We all had our radios on every night, listening to the latest reports. When anyone in the community received a letter from one of their loved ones, word traveled fast. Of course, the really bad news always had a way of making it to your door. As long as you didn't get one of those dreaded telegrams…" Her voice trailed off softly.

"We were having a get-together at the Tabors'," she went on. "It was a beautiful, sunny day, and we had all brought covered dishes. I recall watching the kids running around and playing." I saw a smile slide slightly across her face. "They had been cooped up all winter and were laughing and running around. It felt good to watch them, like for a second, life was normal."

She walked over and took the seat at the island in the kitchen beside me as she described. "I was sitting on the front porch with the rest of the ladies." She cocked her head. "You know how it always goes, the women gather on one side and the men another." She smiled. "They were all talking, but I barely heard what they were saying. I was immersed in watching everybody. I looked out at the crowd gathered around the front lawn. Folks came from all over Cumberland County, at least the southern parts like Vandever, Winesap, and Midway."

She got that distant look in her eye I was becoming familiar with. "I was watching your uncle Paul. He was just a young boy," she continued. "And I thought, I can relate to that little fellow. Sickly, I had heard everyone say. I thought he probably heard the same words I had always heard from doctors and adults alike. Maybe not quite to the extent I had heard them, but I wasn't sure. No one had said what was wrong with him if they knew. I know he spent a lot of days in bed, going to doctors, and was often on prayer lists. He looked pale and was a skinny, little fellow. I felt so sad for him. I knew that he, too, probably, went to bed at night and wondered if he closed his eyes would he get to open them the next morning. Then there would be times that you'd feel so weak and tired…it might be just as well if…" Her voice trailed off as she shrugged her shoulders slightly.

Mama's words broke my heart.

"You wonder always, in the back of your mind, if you will get a chance to do all the things you dream of doing. You try hard to block out those whispers that run a chill up your spine," she described clearly. Then she perked up a bit as she explained, "I noticed he was standing among the grown men instead of running and playing like the other kids. I thought perhaps he was not quite up to it again. Then I saw one of my least favorite neighbors from down the road. The thing about the Tabors, they never excluded anybody. Everyone was always welcome. This fella, though, I had no use for him. You could never believe a word he said."

I saw a familiar look of disapproval on her face as she described this fellow. "He actually punctured his own eardrum with a nail to get out of going into the military. Then he found out they wouldn't have him anyway because of his stupid flat feet!"

"Yikes!" I said, squinting tightly. "That's crazy!"

She nodded her head in agreement. "Right… while the good ones, like your daddy, marched off, eager to do whatever they could. Then I heard that nasty fella yell, 'Boy!' I looked over in his direction, and he had stooped to meet little Paul face-to-face, spewing that nasty chewing tobacco on the poor little fellow. My blood hit an instant boiling point when I heard him say, 'Children are meant to be seen and not heard!'"

She glanced at me before turning to look at the towel she was holding in her lap. "I always hated that statement anyway. I don't remember telling my body to move, but all of a sudden, I felt my feet stomping hard across the wooden porch, down the steps, and heading right toward where they were both standing. I positioned myself between him and Paul, one hand on my hip and the other pointing that loaded mom finger," she turned to face me with her pointer finger sticking straight out, "as you call it."

I laughed knowingly. Her mom finger seemed to hold extra power. If she pulled that out, you'd best do what she said.

"I stood right between that nasty man and that little boy. I heard myself saying angrily, 'Don't you dare talk to him that way! In my opinion, what the kids have to say is usually *way* more interesting and definitely more *truthful*.' I put a very strong emphasis on *truthful*. He stood there, looking at me incredulously and didn't say a word. I turned, took Paul by the hand, and marched him right out of that *man's* way."

Then she gave me a funny look and said, "Out of the corner of my eye, I saw your Pa. He was standing there, arms across his chest. I thought, 'Oh, no! I've done it again!' I was pretty sure I hadn't said any bad words...out loud!"

We both laughed. Then she went on, "I had to really think about it for a second, but I was pretty sure I hadn't. If I did, though, the family name would be tarnished for sure! Just before my heart sank, I saw my dad raise his hand slightly to cover his mouth, hiding a smile. I breathed a sigh of relief and thought, 'Oh, good. He's not mad then. Family reputation might still be intact.' Then it occurred to me, here I am a grown woman. Married, for goodness' sakes! I wondered then if we ever grow out of *needing* our parents' approval?"

We were both laughing and, in unison, looked at each other and said, "Nope! Never!" We understood each other completely.

"Then," she continued, "I led Paul just slightly out of earshot, and I stooped to meet him face-to-face. Mostly I just wanted to make sure he wasn't covered in tobacco spit. He lowered his head, and I asked him, 'Are you all right?' He was nodding his head that he was okay, but he wouldn't look up. Then I caught sight of a big grin he was trying to hide. I thought 'Good, he is unscathed.' I breathed a sigh of relief. Then all of a sudden, he wrapped me in a big, tight, quick hug, and off he went, skipping and running with his siblings. I remember smiling to myself as I retook my seat among the rest of the ladies, who, for a few short minutes, had fallen silent, watching the escapade but then fell back into conversation without missing a beat. No one ever said a word about it, not even Dad."

She twisted her mouth a bit before going on, "I often felt that most folks thought women and children were both supposed to be silent—seen, not heard...opinion-less." She cocked her head slightly to one side. "Well, we all know I would never have fit in that box, and I never wanted to put my kids in it either."

I laughed again and said, "No, Mom, I cannot imagine you *not* expressing your opinion, and I have certainly never known you not to have one!"

That night, driving home, I thought of her story. I pictured Uncle Paul, Daddy's little brother, as a child. To this day, he is one of the sweetest, most stubborn men I have ever known. Of course, you could not be a Tabor without a bold, stubborn streak. He has a farm in Ohio and has lots of stuff around his farm: tools, equipment, assorted other things. Developers decided to go in and build a neighborhood all around and to the back of his property. Then these newcomers decided to start complaining about Uncle Paul's collection of stuff. He was approached about getting rid of it or moving it to appease the new neighbors. In his uniquely humble, sweet, calm voice and manner, he simply explained he understood where they were comin' from and all, but he was there before they got there, and he really liked all his stuff to be just right where it was at. He explained it so kindly that no one was able to get mad at him or make him do what they wanted.

So they approached the mayor. The mayor then came to his house, and again, Uncle Paul, in his sweet, calm demeanor, explained that all his stuff was right where it was when that new development came to be, and although he understood how they felt, he really liked everything he had right where it was. In the end, everyone loved him and decided his stuff could stay exactly as he had it. The way he talked and his manner always reminded me of Dick Van Dyke's brother on his old show. However, Uncle Paul, even though he was the poster child of humble and kind, was definitely not a pushover.

Then I thought *meek*. That's it. "Meek," I whispered it out loud to myself, feeling the word roll off my tongue. He was the meekest human I have ever known. If indeed "the meek shall inherit the earth," Uncle Paul must have gotten quite an inheritance when he left us.

CHAPTER 11

Tim

I had been working on my Christmas project for some time, collecting stories from both Momma and Daddy. This had turned out to be quite an interesting adventure. I wondered why I had never thought to do it before. As I sat at on a stool, I took a good look around at the all-too-familiar home. So many memories. Tim had cut lumber and replaced the carpet with hardwood flooring. The double oven was the original from the early seventies and was still the best oven I had ever seen, a great example of "they don't make them like they used to." The kitchen and dining area was separated by a curved island with eight stools. That open area was great for a big family, having enough room for everyone to gather. Momma always said the kitchen was the heart of the home.

Of course, we needed a lot of room to square dance and polka. I realized at that moment the house was strangely quiet. It had always been bustling with small children and lots of activity. Among the six of us, there were nineteen grandkids. I do not remember a time when we didn't have at least one baby in the house. I liked it better bustling.

As I contemplated these things, I heard the front door open and then slowly close. I recognized the footsteps—heavy cowboy boots, slow and steady. Unmistakable. I heard them stop in front of Daddy and make a slight pause. He was asleep in the living room. Then softer, steadier steps moved across to Momma's chair. I heard low whispers between them. Without seeing, I knew he was bending to kiss her cheek, as usual. She was in her reading chair. I turned as Tim made his way around the wall into the kitchen.

He spotted me at the counter. In a low but almost excited tone, or as excited as he ever got, at least, he said with a big grin, "I got a story about Daddy for ya."

"Really?" I said, all ears. I could tell by his demeanor it must be a good one.

He took the stool beside me. At this point, my project was not a secret, but what was in it would certainly be a surprise. "Well, I got rained out of work early today…" he started. Tim was in the construction business and specialized in concrete work. "And on the way home, I decided to stop at Murphy's for a beer."

Murphy's Bar and Grill was located between our house and town on Lantana Road. It was a local hangout that always looked a little sketchy to me, just the kind of place I'd look for Tim if he ever went missing, though. I pictured Tim striding though this divey little bar, made out of a single-wide trailer, as he began.

"Anyway, when I walked in, it was about midday, so there weren't but one other feller in there, sittin' at the bar. I noticed he was an older fella. As I was walking up to the bar, the bartender looked up and said, 'Well, Tim Tabor, what can I get fer ya?'

"I noticed the odd look the other feller gave me when the bartender said my name. He turned around real sharp-like," he explained. "I was tryin' to figure out if I knew him, but if I did, I sure couldn't place him. He kept lookin' at me, starin', I'd say. I was about to get uncomfortable and thought about asking him what he was up to when he finally moved to the stool beside me. He said, 'So your last name is Tabor?' I thought fer a second I might ought to deny it but couldn't figure out why, so I just said, 'Yes, sir, I'm Tim Tabor. Do I know you?' I offered my hand, and he shook it, so I knew then he'd be more friend than foe.

"We both took a sip while I waited for him to say what was on his mind. He hesitated a little and then asked if I was related to a Marshall Tabor. I said, 'As a matter of fact, he's my dad. Do you know him?' He said, 'Son, your dad saved my life once.' Then he reached down and pulled out his wallet and said, 'Let me pay for your beer, and I'll tell ya all about it.' I just said, 'Aaaaaawwwwww haaaaiiiiilllll, ya don't say.'"

Translation (from Tim to *normal* English, that is), "What?" I laughed at Tim's animation. He was also one not easily ruffled or emotionally driven. Under some of the most stressful circumstances, he usually could stay extremely calm and untethered. I thought of the time he was working on a fence for Momma and Daddy and accidently sawed the top of three fingers off. He calmly wrapped them in a towel and walked over to my sister and said, "I think I need to go to the hospital." She caught sight of the blood-soaked towel and promptly screamed and hit the floor. "You all right?" he asked *calmly* while holding onto the severed fingertips.

The ride itself consisted of him, Daddy, Connie, and Carolina heading north on Lantana Road at breakneck speed. Mom could hug curves like Mario Andretti when she needed to. By the time they reached the hospital, it was a bit hard to tell who needed to be wheeled in first. The guy with blood all over him or his white-as-a-sheet assistants who seemed to be gasping for air. They made it down that fourteen-mile long and winding road in record time, fifteen minutes to the door of the ER. Tim kept reiterating how he was fine and she really didn't have to drive so fast, but of course, it was to no avail. If he felt any pain, he sure didn't show it.

I had to laugh just a little that here he was, all animated and obviously excited about a conversation he had had with a stranger. "So we sat there pert near two hours while he told me about bein' in the war with Daddy. I'd heard about a few of the tales before, like how Daddy had picked up a little boy and a beagle along the way, I guess a few other things." He shrugged.

He gave me a serious look as he said, "Then he told me one I hadn't heard before. While they were in France, the whole troop was stuck and couldn't move because this German plane kept flyin' over and poundin' 'em, keepin' them stuck with no way out. They were hunkered down as much as they could. It was lookin' awfully bleak fer 'em. Every time they'd try to budge, that plane would circle around and come back, firin' constantly. After a while, Daddy got fed up."

Tim gave me a look that said, "We both know Daddy and his patience when it hit its limits."

"So this feller told me, 'Your dad looked over at us and said, just calm as ever, "I'm gettin' real tired of this. Next time he goes back out, I'm gonna set up that .50 cal. and get that guy." His buddy Roscoe tried to tell him he couldn't do that, he'd get killed. But Marshall had made up his mind. So sure enough, the plane flew over and was goin' out to turn around again, and he jumps outta cover and gets that dang gun ready. I heard Roscoe say, "Awe hell, if he's goin', I am too!" So up Roscoe jumped to go out there and help him get ready for that bugger to come back. He said he just knew they were both committin' suicide. Then here that plane came around, headin' back. Right before he got above 'em and could start shootin', your dad took him down with one shot,' he said, holding up a finger for emphasis. 'With a dadgum .50-caliber machine gun! That plane started smokin' and fallin' right out of the sky, and the pilot parachuted out.

'You talk about a bunch of happy fellers! We all jumped out and started runnin' to your dad and huggin' him. I'm pretty sure he got some kind of award for it if I am not mistaken,' he said."

Then Tim told him he knew Daddy had gotten several awards and at least one bronze star. He explained he had never heard what Daddy had done to get them. The stranger had said he'd never seen a man so determined to win a war in his life. He'd explained that he was pretty sure it had something to do with the little French boy he had picked up along the way. He said that poor kid had gotten really attached to Daddy and vice versa. He had frowned as he told Tim Daddy had to leave the boy behind.

Tim continued his story, "He went on to say after the pilot hit ground, he saw Daddy go up to him and take the leather pouch he had with maps and plans in it. Then he took the scarf the pilot had on. For some reason, those German pilots always wore scarves. Dad kept the scarf and gave the pouch to his sergeant. The sergeant took all the papers out of it and handed the empty pouch back to Dad and told him he could keep it as a souvenir."

"Wow," I said. "Daddy hasn't mentioned that story." While I was pondering that, another thought occurred. "So you had never seen that guy before?"

"No, that's the first time."

I looked at him and said, "I sure am glad you got rained out today."

"Me too." Tim's big white cowboy hat bobbed slightly.

It seemed unlikely, and yet a blessing came from a bar. *Murphy's, of all places*, I mused. *Hmmmmm, who would've thunk?*

CHAPTER 12

Christine and the Family Reunion

I woke up even more excited than usual. I was always excited about going to the family reunion, but that year more than ever. That year we were set to gather at the pavilion overlooking the lake at Cumberland Mountain Retreat. There was a playground for the little ones and a sandy beach and swimming area. Of course, that swinging bridge was always fun for everybody.

Part of the pavilion was open air and part had an enclosed area with a kitchen. We set up all the food inside. Crock pots were plugged in, the refrigerator was filled with goodies and deserts, and coolers were filled with an assortment of drinks and ice.

I love my cousins and aunts and uncles. I usually only saw most of them once a year, barring any tragedies. That thought made me a little sad. I wondered why we did that, only got together for the annual reunion and, of course, at funerals or hospitals. It occurred to me there was some real wasted time in between somewhere. Of course, as families go these days, everyone was spread out across the country. Working, busy, always busy.

We pulled onto the hill overlooking the lake and parked in the grassy area close to the pavilion. We actually had a few weddings there in times past. It was a pretty view. I saw lots and lots of people gathering with dishes and starting to set the food up. We parked, and I gathered my casserole and instructed the children to help with the cases of water. As we got close, we were greeted with lots of hugs and smiles one after the other as we made our way to the serving area. I looked around and spied Aunt Chris. She was talking with Uncle Paul and Daddy and Aunt Rosemary, Paul's wife.

I was very excited at the thought of getting her perspective. I wanted to ask her what all she remembered about their childhood, especially about the time Daddy and Hershel were so far away. She would have been about sixteen to eighteen years old during those years. She would be able to tell me a lot about that time, I thought, and hopefully shed some light on what was going on this side of the pond, maybe tell me a little about Grandma and Grandpa.

Grandma Tabor died when I was only two, so I don't remember her at all. I wish I could have gotten to know her. Everything I ever heard about her was really fascinating. I knew she was a very strong person and quite intuitive. She had to have been a very strong-willed woman to raise all those kids and take care of Grandpa in his half-broken state. Grandpa lived a bit longer, but I was still very young, and all I remember is watching him play his French harp. He really got into it! Reminded me of Grandpa Jones on *Hee Haw.* He would dance around and play it with all his heart and soul. You can see my grandparents in all their kids and even the grandkids. From those two rose a tight-knit and strong-willed bunch of people. If anybody dared to mess with one of them, they would get the wrath of the whole bunch. If one had a problem, they could form a cavalry so fast it would make your head swim! You could count on it. They would drop whatever they were doing and come from however far away they happened to be. Nothing was more important than family. Ever.

Grandma and Grandpa, even in his state, did well.

I can only imagine the determination it took for Grandpa to muster up the very best that was left of him to make sure his kids got a firm foundation. They came together each evening at the end of the day, and together, he and Grandma made sure their family knew where true strength and hope came from. I can still see the effects as I look around at the faces gathered there that day. I knew, very well, the losses and heartbreak life had handed out to each and every one of them. They were a fairly open bunch. Most of them were fearless at sharing the great as well as the not-so-great parts of themselves and their lives. That had to come from knowing they were unconditionally loved.

The whole bunch carried a contagious *joy* everywhere they went. Their laughter was like a saving grace sometimes. No one could be in a room with them and not feel it. It was always there, even in the hospitals and funeral homes.

I was abruptly brought out of my reverie as my cousin Sherry bumped me with her elbow and said, "Suni, where are you, girl?" She was smiling.

"Right here, Ms. Sherry," I answered emphatically. "*Right* here," I whispered again under my breath as I took it all in. Yes, Christine would be a fantastic source of information. I know I was smiling, and I saw the look of "What?" on Sherry's face.

I heard Keilah say, "Mom, can I take Drake down and play on the beach and swim?" I said sure since I had a good, clear view of them. I recalled so many great memories playing in that lake. I'm sure I swam all over it a time or two. I made my rounds with hugs and greetings.

After a bit, I saw my aunts Chris, Mattie, Helen, Polly, Margie, Willene, and JoAnn all sitting together at a table. That was a good group to get in with, I thought. They might all have a bit of input.

I walked over and squeezed into the middle of the group. "Is this the cool kids' table?" I asked, smiling. They laughed.

Polly said, "Of course it is!"

"Well, I've never gotten to sit with the cool kids before. This'll be a first!" I took a seat. I imagined them in school. They all had a Tabor look: high cheekbones, naturally tanned skin (some darker than others), slim, cute figures, long legs. I'd bet they were beautiful, but then, I corrected my thoughts as if someone was listening. They *are* beautiful! Momma always said Christine carried herself like a model, very elegantly. I could tell they were all siblings, for sure.

We made our plates and were busy filling our mouths with BBQ and/or fried chicken, baked beans, and personally, I put a dollop of each homemade casserole on my plate so I could try everybody's. You may have figured out at this point, eating is my number 1 hobby. Plus, it was all about being fair and trying everybody's, right?

Then I turned my attention back to the ladies beside me. They were already talking about things in the past. It would definitely not take a lot of prodding to get them to share their memories. "Hey, guys, I was wondering if you could tell me a little about what it was like when you were kids and maybe a little about the time when Daddy and Hershel were away in the war? Daddy has been telling me some of his WWII stories, and I was thinking, if you guys don't mind, maybe fill me in on what you were going through at that time. Maybe even give me some insight on Grandma and Grandpa?" I asked my questions with raised eyebrows while simultaneously lifting a spoon laden with something wonderful.

Mattie was the first to speak up, "I remember how quiet it got after they were gone. I think that was the hardest part." All their heads bobbed a little in unison.

I remembered that quiet after Tony died. "I understand," I said.

Then Aunt Chris picked up. "Momma and Daddy were so on edge. Marshall was only fourteen and Hershel nearing sixteen when they went up north to Ohio together and got jobs for a while. Those two were always inseparable. They came back right before Hershel got drafted," Chris said.

"Can you imagine us letting our kids take off from home that young?" Mattie said.

Then Chris added, "Yeah, but things were so different then." Aunt Chris brightened a bit and said, "Remember when Mom and Ruby made us new dresses?"

While giggling, the girls all said, "Yes! We thought we were something."

I loved watching them together. They were always full of giggles.

Helen said, "It had been a while since we had anything new, and that Ruby made matching cloaks and had us decked out like movie stars."

"I remember that, and I was only about six!" Margie added.

I took another bite of a delicious potato casserole and wondered who made that dish.

"Mom was smart like that, ya know," Christine said while looking at her sisters. They were nodding their heads in agreement. "She knew how to keep spirits up and, of course, bring everyone together." She looked directly at me then. I knew she meant Mom. She was bringing Mom into the family then, like Mom had told me. Chris paused a moment and took a bite. "Mom would bring everybody together on regular intervals to pray for the boys. She always knew if they were in immediate danger or if they were fairly safe. She was in touch with all of us on a level I could never quite understand. You definitely could not get anything past her." They all laughed again. I got the sense they might have tried a time or two.

Then Mattie chimed in. "Do you remember that young French fellow that came lookin' for Marshall?" She looked over at Chris.

Chris's eyes widened. "Oh, yeah! I almost forgot! It was on a Sunday because everybody was at the church except for me. I was working at the diner in town," she said excitedly before going on to explain. "A young Frenchman with a heavy accent stood out in Crossville!" She laughed again. "He stopped in the diner and was asking where to find Marshall Tabor, but no one could understand him. I heard him as I was walking out of the kitchen with some plates of food. He was talking to Nancy, the other waitress I worked with. I looked over, and she was nodding, looking confused. I could tell she was not understanding him at all. I set the plates down in front of the guests I was serving and walked over to see if I could help. Then I heard him say Marshall Tabor. I looked at him and asked in my thick Southern accent, 'You're looking for Marshall Tabor?' He smiled real big and said, 'Yes! Marshall Tabor.' I said, 'He is my brother. I can help you.' He stretched his hand out, grabbed mine, and kissed it. I laughed and said, 'Let me finish up here, and I will lead you to him. If I try to give you directions, you would just get lost, I'm sure!' He seemed to understand us way better than we understood him because he nodded in agreement."

She took a few more bites and continued, "The little church we went to was way out in Vandever, close to the farm. Lantana Road as well as Vandever Road were gravel all the way then. I think it was about fourteen miles from town. In those days, goin' into town was a big deal. You didn't go unless you had to. We usually only made it about once a week, at least up until I started workin' at the diner. That was just part-time. I still had to help Mom with everything at the house and farm." She looked out as if remembering the way of life then. "You could drive the whole way and not see another car most of the time. If you did have trouble of any sort, the next car coming by was probably someone you knew, a neighbor or relative."

She looked at me and smiled. "That has definitely changed. It's a busy, paved highway now, at least compared to what it used to be." She seemed to remember what she had been telling me about and caught her breath and said, "Anyway, I knew he'd never find it and I had better lead him to Marshall. Plus, I was very curious as to who he was and what he wanted with my brother. I went to the back and took off my apron and hung it up. I asked Nancy if she minded if I went ahead and left. She didn't care. We were never busy on Sundays in those days. Most folks gathered at their homes for a big dinner after church. Mom always had a big Thanksgiving-style Sunday dinner for whoever wanted to come over. Most of the time, it would be the whole congregation.

"That poor Frenchman was very excited that he had finally found someone who could take him to Marshall. Apparently, he had stopped at the gas station, and they had just pointed him toward the diner. My way, I suppose. He was trying to explain to me how Marshall had helped him during the war with his cat as we walked out to our cars. I couldn't quite make out what that was all about. I had heard Marshall talk about his dog, Schnapps. He'd never mentioned a cat that I had heard, at least. I was not entirely surprised, I guess. I'm sure if there was a cat that needed saving, he'd have done that too!" We all laughed again.

"Sounds like Marshall, rescuing animals and kids," Margie chimed in.

Then Chris began again, "I drove slow as not to lose him. I was afraid he might give up. It was so far out. Then, I thought, he came all the way across the Atlantic. I guess he'll hang in there until we get to Vandever!" Christine smiled recalling the scene.

Margie said, "That is something, isn't it? The fact that he came back after, what, about six years just to look Marshall up?" She gave Chris a quizzical look.

"Amazing," I said.

Chris continued, "When we pulled up to the church, the doors were opening up. Service had just ended. I stopped my car and got out. I waited for him to walk up beside me, and I said, 'He will be coming out any minute.' I pointed to the opening doors on the front of the little white church.

"We started walking toward the door, and I saw Marshall and Ruby at the top of the steps, walking out. Mr. Frenchman, I will call him, because I can't remember his name, and I'm not real sure I ever caught it," she said wrinkling her nose. "He went walking up to Marshall. I was right behind him. When he got close, I watched Marshall's face. He looked confused. Then Mr. Frenchman just said, 'Marshall, do you know who I am?' Everyone got really quiet, waiting to see what was happening. I could see the searching in Marshall's face. He did not recognize this man. I heard him say it out loud then, 'No, sir, I don't believe I do.' Then I watched as Mr. Frenchman pulled a scarf from his coat pocket. You should've seen Marshall's face." She got a little teary-eyed recalling. "He was so shocked…*awed* might be a better word. His eyes welled up a bit before he caught it. He couldn't speak. I saw the flood of recognition come across his face. I still was not sure what I had just witnessed. I knew I would never forget it, though. Later, I heard Marshall say as soon as he saw that scarf, he saw that little boy's face, just as plain as day." They stood there for a few seconds and then wrapped each other in a hug. They had shared an experience that was beyond words. For that young man, Marshall may as well have been superman."

She looked at me with a sideways grin. "Marshall would say he just helped him catch his cat and get back home safely. For that little boy, at that time, witnessing a simple act of kindness in the middle of a war-torn city, it was hope. I can only imagine that an American uniform must have looked like a superhero outfit to him. Marshall's calm and soothing smile was probably better than any cape could possibly be." She looked over at Daddy as he was smiling and talking and then gave me a wink as if to say "See?"

Yep, that I understand. We all sat there, silently contemplating, visualizing this reunion so long ago. Then I asked, "Did you ever get the whole story of what happened exactly?"

"Yeah, I asked Marshall." Then she looked at me and went on, "Come to find out, Marshall had been given a few days leave to go into Paris for the weekend. Control of Paris had been taken back by the Allies. Marshall described it as a city that had gotten a new lease on life and was trying to get back to some form of *normal*. There was still uneasiness, of course. The war had not actually ended yet. Tension was still hanging in the air as if the monster might return at any moment. The Allies were on Hitler's heels, for sure, but the war was not won yet. Hopes were high, and *that* can make all the difference in the world.

"Anyway, he was walking through the city, just taking in the scenery, when suddenly he saw a little boy, about eleven or twelve, he guessed. He had a bag of groceries in each hand yet was trying to chase his cat down as it was obviously making a break for it." She laughed again. "He just reached down and scooped up the cat. He then told the boy he'd help him get his armload home. The boy led him just a few blocks to an apartment where he lived. He ran into his house, rattling something off in French to his parents. Marshall could hear him as he stood outside the door. He was holding the cat and one of the bags of groceries, waiting for his parents to come to the door. The parents were very leery because German soldiers had been posing as Americans trying to get into homes to try and get information. They walked slowly and carefully to the door and were going to send Marshall away. He could see how nervous and scared they were. The father came to the door slowly. As he was approaching, Marshall opened his mouth and spoke. He just said something simple, like 'Howdy there, I'm Marshall Tabor. I was just helping your boy get home with his cat…" I can imagine him trying to hand his armful back to them." She was laughing at that point. Then she added, "That was all it took. They knew immediately he was all American! They smiled and gave him a look of sheer relief, knowing he was not a German spy. No one could fake that accent! They were so excited and obviously relieved, they invited him in to have dinner with them. By the end of the evening, the boy told Marshall that when he grew up, he would come to America and find him. Marshall smiled but didn't take him seriously. He then thanked them for their hospitality and the dinner. He turned to the boy and gave him the scarf he had taken off the German pilot of the plane he had shot down. Told him it was something to remember him by and said something like 'Good luck keeping up with your cat.'"

Chris paused there to see if I knew what she was referring to regarding the plane. I smiled and acknowledged I knew about that particular incident.

"Daddy must have been very surprised that the little Frenchman was so serious about looking him up, huh? Comin' all the way to…well, not just America, not to New York or someplace easy to get to, but all the way to Vandever in Crossville, Tennessee! Of all places…" I said with amazement. Wow.

Then Aunt Chris said, "He had no idea what an impression he had made."

I replied, "I don't think he ever does." I took a breath and said with more conviction, "He doesn't have a clue, I don't think, the impression he makes on people." I thought of yet another little boy who had crossed his path in the midst of that war as I sent up another little prayer.

Then I told Aunt Christine that I had only recently heard about the plane he shot down. Oddly, it had come from a strange man in a dive bar. She gave me an odd, rather wide-eyed look. "Oh," I explained quickly, "I was *not* in the dive bar with the strange man." Then hastily I pointed in Tim's direction.

We all broke out in another fit of giggles. "That makes a little more sense," Mattie said.

Whew, reputation saved.

CHAPTER 13

Shipwreck

"The farther we got out to sea, the rougher the water got. About the third night, I was tryin' to sleep but was rocked back and forth and swingin' so hard sleep was impossible. I 'bout got bucked right out of the bed. Several guys were sick at that point. The smell was awful. I finally gave up and got up. I decided to try and get up on deck and get some air. Walking out, I had to hold onto the poles. I got to the steps and was knocked from side to side as I held onto the rails tryin' to work my way to the top. I remember the water sloshing and running down the stairs toward me. I started gettin' real worried and wanted to see what was goin' on up there. I held tight and made my way to the top.

"It was really dark and hard to see, but about the time I stepped up to the top onto the deck, a big streak of lightning lit up a giant wall of water. I had to crane my neck back to find the top of the mountain of a wave. It looked like a big ball of fire comin' right at us. It was the most incredible thing I had ever seen, several feet above the ship and growing fast. I stood in awe, couldn't believe what I was seein'. I remember thinkin', how could that be real! I was frozen in my footsteps, completely unable to move. Then I heard someone yell, 'Get below deck now!' Right about that time the wave hit.

"It seemed like everything started movin' in slow motion. Out of the corner of my eye, I saw flailing arms and legs flying through the air, disappearing out into that big black hole. I heard yelling and bloodcurdling screams. I couldn't move. Suddenly, I felt my breath getting knocked right out of me by a cold, hard force stronger than I could ever have imagined. Then I too was flyin' off my feet and through the air. It still felt like I was moving in slow motion, and I could see everything that was happening so clearly as if I was above it all just watching…helplessly watching. I saw faces as they were pushed away, out to sea." He hung his head. "There was nothin' anybody could do."

I took a deep, sudden breath. It seemed to bring us both back to where we were, safely in our home, in the present time. I know my eyes were wide and teary, and I felt myself shaking as I laid my hand on his and wrapped my fingers around. All I could get out of my mouth was "Oh, Daddy."

He seemed to snap out of a trance and went on, "I landed back down at the bottom of the steps, flat on my back. My breath was knocked out of me, and I was under about three feet or so of water. I remember somebody grabbing my arm and pulling me to my feet and asking if I was okay. I couldn't catch my breath to answer. I think he drug me back to the bunk room and said to hold on. The ship was rolling and bucking like a wild bull. I wrapped myself around the pole. All you could do was hold tight. It was so loud you couldn't hear each other. The life-boats were beating against the hull and sounded like they were going to break in the wall. Most of them got knocked loose and swept away. The galley got hit hard, and the equipment in the kitchen was knocked loose and sliding back and forth, beating the walls on the inside. The ship was popping and cracking and sounded like it was breaking in two. It seemed to go on for hours."

He took a deep breath and a small sip of moon-shine I had poured us. "When it finally settled down, it was daylight, cloudy and foggy, but you could see the damage. The ship was broken, and we could only maneuver through parts of it. We had taken on a lot of water and had to wade through it to get to the mess room where there was some food. A lot of it was soggy but edible enough to keep us alive. There was a lot of men missing. We couldn't tell right then how many. Those of us who were still in one piece knew we had just gotten real lucky, but things still looked pretty bleak. We had no way of callin' for help, and unless a miracle occurred, nobody would ever find us."

He gave me a weak grin and then added that the storms came and went over the next twenty-two days. "Every time it started again, we figured that'd be the end," he said. More than once, I listened to him repeat, "I don't understand how that ship didn't sink. It was broken in two, and half of it was underwater." He looked down and shook his head as he said, "We had 'bout given up. The chaplain had told us to get ourselves right with God. It didn't look good."

He looked up again with a little gleam in his eye as if he was standing on that ship once again, looking out…at hope. "But hope manifested right out of sea and air, floating out so far you could barely see it with the naked eye. The USS *Enterprise*. It was carrying more troops home from Europe to the United States when they spotted us. They couldn't bring their large ship any closer because the water was so rough. They had to send over their smaller rescue boats. They attached ropes to our ship to scale across to get to the smaller vessels. Wind was whippin' and the waves were rough and knocked everybody around trying to make it across.

"I remember sayin' to a fella that was getting hold of the rope to hang on tight as he could…that he could do it. I was tryin' hard to believe my own words. He would have to hang on tight or he'd end up blown out to sea just like several others had already. We all heard their screams as they were swept out to sea. It was the most helpless I had ever felt. There was nothin' you could do for 'em. When lightning would strike, you'd get a second's glimpse of what you were up against. I'd have liked it better if it'd just stayed dark, I think."

I was torn between worry that this was dredging up too much of a painful past and wanting to understand what he had gone through. But I wanted my kids, my grandkids, to understand what had transpired so long ago that made it possible for them to live this life. I wanted his life of sheer guts and determination to be something they could hold onto someday. So I didn't stop him as he kept going.

"They had been at it for hours. I had no idea how long, really. Those men risked their lives every time they made another trip to get more of us. They would not give up until they had saved every last one they could, though."

I could scarcely breath with the vision in my mind. He had to be so frail and weak. He'd just recently snuck out of a hospital with hepatitis. He'd been cold and starving for twenty-two days. I sipped my little thimble of moonshine, trying not to make a sound so as not to distract him.

"With every one that made it across, we had a bit more hope. I told Roscoe to go ahead of me. Again, I whispered to God and Roscoe at the same time, 'Hold on tight.' With that, he was gone. He was working his way toward the rescue boat. It was not a good plan, per se, but it was the only plan we had. Each man would get off our broken, half-sunk ship and hang onto the rope against incredibly strong winds with waves, cold and hard as ice, trying to knock him loose until he made it to safety. We had already seen several lose the battle. I was soaked to the bone. We all were. I assume the water must be really cold, but I couldn't feel a thing. That was good, I reckoned. One after the other, one after the other, one after the other. The boat we were on was rocking and cracking and splitting. I kept thinking it was just going to give and then we'd be done for sure. Any minute. Just one more. The storm had no mercy. It had been coming and going for near a month. When it went, it just settled enough to give us a little break, but then it would come back as fierce as ever.

"I had made it through most of that war, barely, I guess. It almost struck me as funny for just a moment that instead of being killed by a bullet or a bomb, it'd be a darned ol' storm. It was just on the verge of comical."

He turned toward me with a sad grin. "There were times, small moments, even I had 'bout given up. I thought of Allon. We had gone through boot camp together. He was from close to the same area I was from in Middle Tennessee. All he ever talked about was his mother. He really loved his mother. From the very beginning, he had told me he would not make it through this war and made me promise to contact his mother and let her know what happened to him. I tried to tell him not to think like that. He didn't listen, though. He was so sure of his fate. I have no idea why. Then, sure 'nuff, it happened. He was shot on the battlefield. I saw him go down, and without a second thought, I ran over to him. Bullets were flyin' all around, but I wasn't really thinking at that moment. I plopped down on my knees and put my arm under his head and lifted him up. I was goin' to carry him somewhere safe and get help, but then I noticed his bowels were coming right out of him. I knew it wasn't any use, so I just stayed there and held him. He looked up at me and one last time in a low whisper said, 'Promise you'll go see her.' I tried to say something but couldn't get the words to come out, so I just nodded my head yes. It was enough, I guess, for him to feel peaceful about letting go. He died right in my arms. I have no idea how long I was there or how I didn't get hit. Next thing I knew, Roscoe was beside me, his hand on my shoulder. 'Marshall, we need to move,' he said." Daddy jumped a little and said, "I heard that again. 'Marshall, you need to move. It's your turn.'

"My stomach lurched a little. I knew I was physically at the weakest point I had ever been in my life. I had been more than just a little sick. It had taken its toll on my body. I tried to take a deep breath as I reached out and grabbed hold of the rope. I think my hands were numb. I couldn't feel it hardly. It was a big strong woven rope. It wouldn't break. I knew that for sure. I had just watched it hold bigger men than me. If I could just keep hold of it and not let the waves or wind knock me off, I'd make it home."

I could tell by his dazed expression, he was standing back there once again as if transported through time. I noticed his hands had let go of mine and were clenched tightly as he relived that moment.

"I don't recall exactly what I did first—right hand then left, or was it left then right? My feet were up and crossed over tight at the ankles. You couldn't look at where you were going or you could lose your grip. Just had to tuck in close, hold tight, and move slow. I was movin', tryin' not to think about it too hard and panic, just hold on and move slow."

He took a sudden sharp and shallow breath. "Then I felt a hard wave hit and knock my breath out. My hands slipped and my foot almost came loose. My body was numb, and I couldn't feel my hands. I was losing my grip. The waves felt like hard blocks of ice. They kept comin', one after the other. I was knocked around and knew for sure I wasn't gonna make it. The wind was whippin' so strong I was slippin' and almost fell when I felt somethin' sweep across my face. It felt warm and soft. I smelled a familiar scent, like perfume. My eyes had been squeezed shut, but right then, I opened 'em. That's when I saw…" His voice trailed off. "At first, I thought I was dreamin', but I could still feel the wind and the spray of water."

He silenced a moment, and I realized I was holding my breath. I barely whispered, "What was it, Daddy?"

He smiled slightly and said, "I saw just a light wisp of red hair floating slowly right in front of me. Then she turned to face me with those bright-blue eyes, lookin' right at me, smilin'. All of a sudden, I felt strong hands grabbin' and pullin' me in. I had made it. I couldn't remember gettin' across. I just remembered seeing her and knowing I would make it home."

He looked at me and grinned and said, "I ain't never told that to anybody before." We both sat there with tear-filled eyes.

Then I asked, "Do you mind if I tell…everybody?" He didn't say I couldn't.

CHAPTER 14

Rescued

"Next thing I knew, I was on the USS *Enterprise* headin' home. I must have been out of it for a while. I don't remember gettin' from one boat to the other. I don't remember how I got to the room or in the bed. I do remember someone feedin' me hot broth. I'd wake up ever' now and then to swallow what was bein' put in my mouth. It felt like heaven goin' down my throat. That's about all I remember until we pulled in to port.

"Roscoe said, 'Marshall, you able to get up?' I knew if I didn't pull myself together, I'd be forced back into a hospital. So I got up and, as best I could, tried not to look too sickly. We all had to weigh in and get looked at by the Army doctor. I was worried about gettin' past him. When we got off the ship, we lined up and took our turn. I remember the look on his face when he saw me. Of course, the first words out of his mouth were, 'Son, you need to go straight to the hospital.'

"I said, 'No, sir. I thank ya for your concern, but I've had a right hard time gettin' here, and I'm goin' home now.' He just stood there a minute, starin'. Then he shook his head and said, 'Well, son, I sure hope you make it.'

"We were loaded up on busses and taken to the Greyhound Station. I couldn't believe I was finally on my way home. It seemed like it had been forever. I calculated in my head by that time the next day, I should be in Tennessee."

He got a curious look on his face and said, "That is until we arrived at the bus station. It had been snowin' hard for a while, and the roads were solid ice. I actually hadn't paid no mind until I saw all the GIs that were crowded in the station. The busses had all been cancelled or delayed. There were GIs sleepin' all over the floor, the seats, and benches. Hardly a spot to be had. Some had apparently been there several days. My heart dropped. At that rate, it might've taken a week or more to get home. Especially since the snow was still fallin'. I looked around and walked back outside. It was brisk and cold. Snow filled the sky with no sign of lettin' up anytime soon. At least I was in America, I thought. No horrible odors and ash-filled sky. No battles bein' fought. I noticed all the cabs lined up along the front, letting more folks out. I questioned as to whether any more would fit in the buildin'.

"Then I got an idea. I turned around and went back in. Roscoe was leaned against the wall, talkin' to a few other fellers. I headed straight to him and asked if he'd wanna go in together on a cab and see if they'd take us at least closer to home where we might could pick up a bus further down the line. He straightened up and said, 'Yeah, let's try it!' Another feller heard us talkin' and said he lived in Nashville and wanted to go in on it with us. So the three of us headed back outside. The first cab we spotted was an elderly lady lettin' out some more poor fellers that'd also be stuck there. We asked her if she could take us as far as she could and we'd make the rest of the way on our own. We never thought she would take us all the way to Tennessee. She asked where we lived, and we told her. Then she surprised us by sayin' 'For eighty dollars apiece, I'll take ya right to your doors.' We all looked at each other right curious-like, and me and Roscoe said our doors were a long ways out. Just a little closer'd be good. Then she said very stern, 'You heard me. Eighty dollars apiece, and I'll take ya to your doors!' So we got in.

"Oh, Lord, what a mistake that was. We realized it right quick when we got out onto the road. It was covered in ice and snow, and that woman didn't slow down a bit. She talked nonstop, hands flailin'. Most of the time she was lookin' at us and not payin' a bit of attention to the road. She went wide on turns, and we slid sideways and was all over the road. Thank goodness no one else was on them, but I don't think she even noticed. If she did, she sure didn't let on. Roscoe was in the front, and I heard him tellin' her he'd be glad to drive and give her a break, but she wouldn't hear of it. Finally, he talked her into pullin' over at a diner. We were relieved to stop for a while. We got a little food and coffee. We all tried again to get her to let one of us drive. We told her she looked awful tired. She just said that she was not allowed to let anybody else drive. She was fine, she assured us. I swear I think I was more nervous on that drive than I had been on the ship. I just sat back and closed my eyes real tight. It was a long trip.

"We came through Nashville first and let the other feller off. When he got out, he said, 'Boys, I'll be prayin' for ya.' With that, he was gone. I figured we'd made it that far. Crossville wasn't too far away."

He lowered his head chuckling. "I was the next'n'. We got to Crossville and made it all the way down Lantana Road. She was true to her word and got us to our doors, sure 'nuff."

He got a more serious look in his eyes as he described. "I told her to let me off at the top of the gravel drive. I got out and felt the crunch of snow under my boots. Home never felt so good. The air was crisp and clean. The snow had stopped, but the ground was covered and sparklin' white. The trees were all covered. It looked like a picture, all sparkly. It was about five o'clock in the morning, just before sunrise. I took a good look around, and it all looked as I remembered. Your grandpa Kerley had built the house right before I left. It had green siding made of asphalt shingles, a metal roof, and of course, a wide front porch. I could see smoke comin' out of the chimney and knew it'd be warm inside. I stood there a minute just takin' it all in when I heard hoof steps comin' up to the fence line. There was Ole Joe headin' lickety-split my way. I went over right quick and met him. I swear he had a tear runnin' down his face. He nuzzled me and whinnied. I hugged him back. I was sure proud to see him. It's mighty curious what these animals understand, but I do believe it's way more than we give 'em credit for."

I had to agree.

"I stood there a minute and then headed to the front porch," he continued. "I knocked. I didn't hear anybody up, so I knocked a little harder. I still didn't hear anything, so I tapped the window. I heard movement, steps, a crash of some sort, and then Ruby's voice, I'm pretty sure. After another thump or two, I heard the jiggling of the doorknob and clanking of the keys. I could tell she was havin' trouble getting it open, and I was startin' to get cold."

He paused. "Then the door pulled open, and there she stood. She looked disheveled and… shocked." He hung his head low. "I saw right away she didn't recognize me. I thought then there may not be enough of me left…"

I saw that welling in his eyes again, yet he held it back.

"I finally mustered up the strength to say some-thin'. It came out in a barely recognizable voice. 'Ruby…it's me.'"

CHAPTER 15

He's Home

"Ever since Ms. Tabor had told us Marshall was on a ship that was sinking and we needed to pray, I had been having horrible nightmares. I was torn between hoping she was crazy or confused, to knowing deep down that that was not likely. I'd never known her or her instincts not to right on target," Mom began. "I thought of her whispered promise: 'It will all work out just fine.' She had reiterated that whenever she noticed the worry pop back into my eyes. I was once again playing with baby Jo, kissing her sweet little fingers…wondering. Ms. Tabor's sweet confidence filled me with hope… that is until she told all of us, with confidence, that

Marshall's ship was sinking, adamantly pleading for God to bring him home safely. There was no question. There was no evidence. Just her knowing that he was not just in trouble. He was drowning in a frozen sea. She hadn't called for prayers because he was off fighting a war. She said very specifically he was on a sinking ship. Adamantly. Everyone wondered how she could know such a thing. Everyone knew no matter how hard to explain it would be, that she *did* know."

I watched Mom visibly shudder. "We prayed. We all prayed. When I tried to go to sleep, all I could see was his face underwater."

I shuddered.

"I dreaded sleep," she went on. "The haunting vision was suffocating. I often woke up coughing and choking, trying to catch my breath as if I were the one drowning. I'd pray again and some more and again. Just as my body was about to give in to complete exhaustion, I heard something. I opened my eyes with a jerk. My feet hit the floor before I comprehended what I had actually heard. Was it a knock at the door? Maybe Mom or Dad had gotten up. Then I heard it again, a tap, tap, tap on the window of the front door. I grabbed a smaller blanket at the foot of my bed and quickly wrapped it around my shoulders and ran toward the living room. As I entered, my toe hit the corner of the coffee table. I shrieked, and well, I think I said 'Shit' at the top of my lungs. I started hobbling and holding my foot, and I heard it again, louder, more adamant that time.

"Who could it be? Could he be home? Maybe, or it could be someone with news. So early in the morning, it could be bad news. Or…I grabbed the skeleton key above the door and tried to put it through that small hole in the knob. Did it get smaller? My hands were shaking, and I was having a hard time working it. You have to, first off, get the key in that darn small hole, then press in just the right spot, just the right way…and darn it! My hands would not cooperate! I tried to calm myself. Whoever it was, was probably frozen to the porch by then. 'Please let it be good news!' I whispered just under my breath. 'Lord, please let it be good.' Do I dare hope? Would it be too much to ask? I heard a click, click, and the knob finally turned. 'Thank goodness!' I said to myself as I pulled the door back, and in one sweep of the hand, I turned the switch for the front porch light."

She paused and blinked her eyes as if still trying to clear her vision. "I stopped. Dead still. 'Who?' That thought did not fully form when the next one hit. 'Oh, my Lord, what did they do to you?' I heard the words going through my brain, but I couldn't move. I tried to will my tongue to work. 'Say something,' my brain was screaming.

"I heard my name. I heard his voice. This is real. This *is* real. Finally, the voices in my head seemed to wake me from my trance. I felt my body move forward, and I wrapped my arms around him. I held on lest it be a vision and he might disappear, just like he did when I saw him through Ole Joe's eyes. I felt every bone in his frail body. His skin barely stretched over the protruding bones. I could feel his heart beating. Tears began to roll down my face, quietly at first. Tears of joy, tears of fear, tears of sorrow. When he had left, he had soft cheeks and strong arms. Now, he looked so pale, so sick. I felt his arms wrap around me. Out of nowhere, I heard footsteps from behind and more arms wrapped around the two of us. Mom and Dad had come out and joined in. They started crying, and I gave way to all the tears I'd ever held onto in my life. I turned and kissed his cheeks and then took a good look. He was still standing solidly in front of me. That's all we needed. 'We will be okay from here,' I vowed."

Fresh tears were rolling down her cheek. "He looked at me and gave me *that* grin,' she said whimsically. "All I could think was 'You are going to be okay. I will fix you.'"

*****

Officially, Daddy was not yet home for good. He was given an extended leave to recuperate before going to the Pacific side. He had weighed in at only eighty-nine pounds.

Before he was able to return to duty, American Bomber B-29 deployed the world's first atomic bomb on Hiroshima and Nagasaki, Japan, on August 6, 1945. WWII ended on September 2, 1945.

It was the end of one of the most brutal and deadly wars in modern history. After all was said and done, there were approximately 70 to 85 million lives lost with another 19 to 28 million that died from war-related diseases and famine. Approximately 416,000 were American soldiers.

And yes, for any of those called to duty during that war, every day they lived past the age of eighteen was nothing short of a miracle.

CHAPTER 16

Fairfield Glade

I remember us piling up in the van and strapping Drake, my youngest (only two then), in his car seat. I heard Scott, my husband, say to the rest of the kids, "Buckle up, guys!" I smiled to myself, knowing that he was excited too. I felt really lucky to have a husband that loved my family as much as I do. We consisted of Derek, aged fourteen; Caleb, twelve; Keilah, ten; and as previously stated, baby Drake. Oh yeah, and Scott and me.

We were on our way to the stables Daddy ran at the Cumberland Mountain State Park. From there we planned to load up wagons, saddle up horses, and go for an all-day ride.

Momma, of course, still would not ride a horse. She loved riding the surrey, though, as she called it. That's a fancy name for a wagon, yet it *was* a bit of a fancy wagon. It had one seat built for two. It was covered with a red canvas top and black fringe around the edges. The wagon itself was painted a high-gloss black. The metal wheels and spokes were a bright cherry red to match the top. Daddy had restored it himself. He loved playing with wagons and had a few. Momma loved that one because it was elegant and quite comfortable for a wagon. Daddy had two Belgium horses named Barney and Cindy he would hook up to pull it.

We would ride all day, stop somewhere along a creek or out in a field, and eat whatever we had packed in coolers. Daddy always took cans of sardines with hot mustard and crackers. I think he'd have been happy eating that at every meal. Most folks were not so enthusiastic about that diet. I smiled to myself as I thought I didn't care if we ate Aunt Christine's gritty bologna.

Hopping into the passenger side and sliding my buckle on, I heard Scott say, "You have that smirky smile goin' again. What are you thinkin'?"

I laughed and said simply, "Oh, nothin'. Just excited."

As we began to roll toward the highway, I pulled out a binder filled with various music CDs. With a four-and-a-half-hour drive, we definitely needed music. To be fair, I gave everyone a chance to pick their favorite. We could put in six CDs at a time and hit shuffle.

"Okay, what do you guys want to hear?" I said as I turned to look back at the kids.

The boys broke out simultaneously in a loud chorus. "Pixies!"

I looked at Scott, and he was grinning proudly. Keilah chimed in, choosing the *Real Genius* soundtrack. As a family, we had watched the movie *Real Genius* enough times that we all knew the dialogue by heart. Yet we still laughed as if we'd never seen it before every time the popcorn busted down the evil professor's house.

I gathered the CD's, put them in each slot, and hit shuffle. We anxiously awaited to see whose song choice would play first.

We listened as the player made its familiar *whh-hhhheeerrrrrr* sound, then a bit of a *grrrrrrrrrrr* as if the CD player was purposely dragging it out suspensefully. Suddenly, there it was. A few short beats, and we knew it was Kei's pick. I looked back to watch her singing along dramatically while moving her head side to side. "Everybody wants to rule the world," she sang as she looked at Drake. He laughed. She was a full eight years older than her baby brother. She was another little momma to him. *Familiar dynamics*, I had thought. Carolina is eight years older than me. Connie, five. Tony was actually sixteen when I was born. Tim and Larry were just steps behind him. Technically, I don't remember sharing the house with Tony. He was a husband and father for as long as I could recall. I barely remember Larry and Tim living at home.

I *do* distinctly recall Larry leaving for Vietnam. A bit of heaviness seeped into my heart at the thought of those years. I was just little, but I remember writing him a letter every day. I could still see those three-cent stamps as I placed them on the envelopes. I was a brownie Girl Scout, and Mom would buy dozens of boxes of cookies and send them to him and his troop. My scout leader must have loved me! Larry said it made him the most popular guy in the paddy fields. That's important.

I could feel the red shag carpet under my knees as Mom and I kneeled every night beside my bed, praying for him to come home safely, prayin' that another horrible war would finally come to an end. Mom told me once that it started about the time he was born. She used to rock him at night and think surely it would be over before he grew up. I must have let out a small sigh because Scott looked over at me questioningly. "What?" he asked.

"Nothing," I said softly. I surmised I must not have much of a poker face. All my random thoughts were apparently pretty visible as they scattered across. "Just thinkin'," I replied. Then I took a breath and started sharing what was on my mind.

"I was just remembering things. Like, the day Larry came home from Vietnam." I looked over to see if he really wanted to hear about it. He seemed to be interested, so I went on. "I had been in school all day, antsy to get home and see him. I was so excited! It was always a long bus ride home, but that day, it took *forever*," I said, drawing out the last word.

I paused to take a short breath as that day came vividly into mind. "I can still hear the sound my feet made, running through the front door and into the kitchen. I stopped, looking around and not spotting him. I breathlessly asked, 'Where is he?' Mom was pulling something out of the oven that smelled…*special* as she turned to face me. 'Downstairs,' she said. 'He should be getting out of the shower any minute.' I noticed her big bright smile. I had not seen it for so long! There was no trace of that dreadful fear she'd fought so hard to hide but never could. The worry lines had eased on her forehead, and she actually looked younger, but mostly, she looked *back*. An invisible weight lifted from my chest.

"I ran downstairs as fast as I could, and about the time my feet hit the floor, he rounded the corner, arms opened wide, and picked me up and swung me through the air. I squeezed hold tightly around his neck and whispered, 'Thank you, God.'

"Years later, I overheard him tell one of our cousins that his job during the war was to crawl on his belly ahead of the troops to check for booby traps."

I shuddered at the thought and was glad we did not know that back then. He'd always told us that he was not in a dangerous place and was in a construction unit that rebuilt buildings that had been destroyed. I wondered now if that even existed. Sounded great at the time. I'm sure Daddy knew better…maybe Momma too."

While pondering that, we were suddenly interrupted as one of *my* songs began to play. I give Scott a "This will just have to wait" look as Carman started blasting through the speakers. Drake always sang along with that particular song. I turned my attention to the mirror in my visor, adjusting it to have a clear view of him in the back. When the song got to the chorus, I saw him jut his little chin in the air, stick his skinny legs straight out, and begin belting, "I wove Jesuuus! Wes, I dooooooooooo," major emphasis on "dooooooooooo." We all started laughing. The older kids hesitated for a short moment, afraid the cool police might be watching. They even took a quick glance around, but then they, too, joined in. Suddenly we were all singing at the top of our lungs, "I wove Jesus; how 'bout youuuuuuuu!"

I love road trips. When the song ended, once again, I got a curious look from my husband. "Oh," I said, still smiling. "Where was I?" So many memories, pictures from the past, good and bad, were hopping through my brain. I tried to still them for a moment and figure out exactly where to begin again. "Did I ever tell you that Daddy, Larry, Tim, and Tony were the first contractors out at Fairfield Glade?" I asked.

He raised an eyebrow in a look of surprise. "No," he answered.

"Yeah, I was only about eleven years old then." I guess I shouldn't have been surprised that it had not come up before. Winesap, as Daddy referred to the southern part of Cumberland County, and Fairfield Glade were at least twenty-five miles apart. They were separated by several other small communities and then, the town center, Crossville. Since Scott had been a part of the family, we had not ventured that way. In fact, I think there might have been an invisible gate we were unable to break through of some sort.

"They were working on the Lakeshore Terrace condo units for Fairfield when Tony got hurt," I continued. "Back then, Fairfield was nothing but woods and a dream. They had an agreement with the original developers to handle all the construction of public buildings and homes. I remember overhearing them talk about building golf courses, pools, and lakes and thinking, 'Way out there in the middle of nowhere?'"

We both laughed, knowing what it had become.

"I doubt anyone envisioned that it would ever be what it is now," I said. "Tony was sick about it, or so he said. All that land was his hunting ground. Their company was called Tabor and Sons Construction. Daddy was very excited because it was a major project. Probably the biggest deal he had gotten yet. I heard him tell Tony there'd be plenty of wilderness left and not to worry."

Thinking back, I could still see Tony's face as he looked at Daddy with that sly Tabor grin that seemed to get handed down easily. Some part of him was excited at the prospect too. "Momma always said Tony had a head for numbers and took care of bidding," I continued. My heart slowed a bit as I recalled how quickly everything had changed.

"Then Tony got hurt. He was in a coma for a year before he passed. Daddy and the boys struggled so hard to keep everything going. I think as long as Tony was alive, they held on to hope and managed to keep their feet movin'. After he was gone, though, our house went from being full of music and fun to an unbearable *silence*. Whispers…hushed tones," I said breathlessly before going on. "It was suffocating. I was sure, at first, that I'd lost my whole family."

Then I perked up a bit, recalling, "Then like a herd of angels from heaven, here came all of my aunts and uncles." I looked over at Scott with a small smile just in case he didn't know who I was talking about, and I clarified, "The Tabors, that is. All of Daddy's brothers and sisters and their spouses. They stayed with us at the house for a few days. I counted fourteen sleeping bags lined up on the living room floor one night. Some brought campers and set them up. I was sleeping in one of those sleeping bags in the living room between Polly and Mattie, if I recall correctly," I said, wrinkling my nose, trying to form the picture correctly in my head.

"I have no idea what happened, but one of them did *something* that got them tickled, and they started laughing. Then everyone got tickled and started laughing. Pretty soon, the whole room was filled again. That's when I knew we would be okay. Eventually.

"I understood, even then, it'd take a while. Daddy was not able to make himself drive down Peavine Road. Momma said that everywhere he looked, on the job site or out at all that land around them, all he saw was the ghost of his firstborn son. That's when Tabor and Sons Construction faded away."

We were coming onto I-40 by then, and I spotted a sign with "Knoxville" on it. A warm feeling rushed through me as I decided there really was no place like home. That very word brought a slight tingle right through my soul.

Don't get me wrong. It's not that I minded living in South Carolina at all. In fact, I liked living there, and I *loved* my job. I was a gate and ticket agent for American Airlines. I stopped that thought for a slight second. *Loved the job?* I asked myself. Well, for sure I *loved* the benefits! Flying free was awesome! I loved wearing the uniform, navy pant or skirt suits with a white cotton blouse. We always wore our standard-issued red-white-and-blue scarf that we'd been taught to do a thousand things with at AA Training Center in Dallas. Yes, we had a scarf-tying class.

My favorite part of that job was getting to the airport bright and early before sunrise. I would do my manifest for the first two flights and then sit at the end of the jet bridge and have my coffee. The view was beautiful. Pretty blue lights strung along the runway, and then a slowly brightening, multicolored southern sunrise would magically begin to appear. It was so peaceful and quiet.

At least until the passengers started coming in, making demands and griping about their seats. I frowned just a little. They really were not *always* difficult. Actually, the job was fun. I *did* love it. I cried the day American announced they would be pulling out of GSP and consequently breaking up with me. They gave me options, of course. Those were Salt Lake City, which wasn't bad but too far away from home; New York, which was great place to visit, but they really couldn't pay me enough to live there; or Hawaii, which is a dream vacation destination but waaaaaayyyyyyyyyy too far from home to live. That settled it then. A breakup it would be.

I must have been smirking again because Scott was giving me a curious look. I wondered briefly if he ever got tired of hearing about my family. I heard Momma's voice in my head saying, "Your Pa always said I had my head in the clouds." I guess I came by it honestly.

I heard the boys all break out in song again. The Pixies were playing, and the car was filled with high-pitched voices singing "Ca-ri-bouuuuuuuuu." I watched them and laughed at their rendition. What followed was a growly sort of something (I don't know that I'd call it singing). "Give me wide ground to run" sounded a bit angry. In unison, we all dug out our lowest, most heavy-metal voice and began to sing loudly in a perfect head-bangin' style. And down the road we rolled.

When things settled again, I crawled back inside my head, thinking about the day ahead of us. Tim had a bigger wagon, so I thought Keilah, Drake, and I would ride with him. Scott and the boys usually liked to ride horses. I smiled quietly, thinking of Tim. Let me try and describe him. People often talked about John Travolta's distinct one-of-a-kind walk. Tim had one of those too. Not like John's exactly but every bit as distinct. I guess it could best be described as a cross between John Travolta's and John Wayne's with a smidge of Clint Eastwood thrown in. It's not really a walk, per se, more of a sssllllooowww swagger. *Confident* is the one word I would use. Somehow, he knew the world would keep on turning just fine 'til he got there, *wherever* it was he might be going. Considering the fact he only had one speed, I hoped whatever he was going to was not on fire. Many of his friends called him the Marlboro Man due to his resemblance to their model on posters and billboards.

I had never seen him without his cowboy hat and boots on, just like our dad, but he was almost a foot taller. It was impossible to have a conversation with him without laughing. He had a slow drawl and dry sense of humor mixed with a bit of cowboy wisdom such as "Ya go to hell fer lyin' same as stealin'" when he heard something he thought was doubtful. If I asked him what he wants for dinner, the response will always be the same: sardines and pancakes. Sounds yummy.

His standard response for almost anything he heard was "Aaaaaawwwww haaiill." Like Daddy, he didn't really cuss, per se, just an "Aaaaawwwwww haaaaaiil" on occasion. Now if I said something he agreed with, I'd hear "I guarrr-an-teeee it." However, I have to say I never heard him raise his voice, always calm, cool, and collected. I loved to ride in his wagon with him. He would say something, never cracking a smile, and I'd laugh so hard I'd almost fall off. I'm sure I looked really silly.

All of a sudden, we all heard a *honk* of a car horn, and everyone turned to our left to see a mirror image of ourselves from the number of heads bobbing and hands waiving right down to the vehicle they were driving. More specifically, it was a Chevy Lumina APV minivan, seafoam green with red pinstripes. We started laughing and waved back emphatically. *Cool, they're probably on their way home too! I love it*, I thought to myself. Sometimes, some things really *are* right in the world.

I couldn't wait to see Connie and Carolina. I hadn't seen them in a month, and I *needed* a sisters' fix. Together, we reminded me of my aunts. Momma would say, "Y'all are just like the Tabor girls, always gigglin' and laughin'." If I ever felt sad, all I needed was a dose of sisters. We definitely would be singing while we rode in the wagon! Not that we knew the real words to the songs or have our mother's talent, but that would never stop us.

Momma would sing to us all the time growing up. One of her favorite songs was "I Want to Be a Cowboy's Sweetheart." She would end with an emphatic, "And I am!" Momma could *really* yodel, and Connie, well, she sure tries. Bless her heart. *I hope she doesn't scare the horses.*

I heard a slight grumble starting with the boys. "It's my turn! You've had it for hours!" Derek said. I gave Caleb a look as I turned to settle the ensuing argument. He knew he was being unfair, but holding tightly to the single Gameboy among them, he said, "Just let me finish this one!"

"Caleb." That's all I said while conjuring up my most stern mom look. He raised his head just slightly, and I saw it. That sly Tabor grin.

Finally, we turned onto a gravel road that would shortly end at our destination. We were all eager to get out of the vehicle. We worked to unbuckle and unleash the children. "Be free, be free," I said whimsically while waving my arms in the air. They laughed and began to run toward the barn.

I saw Daddy near the gate. Scott and I headed toward him. When we got close, I saw him looking unusually pleased about something. Scott and I exchanged a curious glance. "Hey, Marshall!" Scott said.

I walked up to hug him while saying, "Hey, Daddy!" The kids all took turns hugging him and then ran off again. They were always happy to be there with lots of wide-open fields and space to play. Plus, Daddy was a fun grandpa. He had great toys, horses, wagons, four-wheelers, and hunting rifles, all the things little boys loved! Even Kei, come to think of it.

The Cumberland Mountain State Park Stables was situated just off Highway 127 South along the edge of the park, sitting atop a plateau with an approximate two-thousand-foot elevation. It is surrounded by beautiful, often smoky, Tennessee mountains. Smiling, I looked out to see rolling hills and open fields. Then I gave Daddy a curious look and asked him what was on his mind.

I couldn't wait to find out what had him so *pleased*. He propped one foot up on the last rail of the fence, like I had seen him do so many times before, crossing his forearms and resting them on the top rail. He began to explain, "I've put a bid in to run the horse stables in Fairfield Glade," he said, grinning.

"Really?" I was quietly surprised.

He went on with a glint in his eyes. "Yeah, they have a real nice barn." I saw Scott grin with understanding. "I'll be able to put up all my horses there too."

I listened to the conversation. I heard the words *nice barn, good opportunity.*

I heard Scott's voice, "That's good, Marshall." However, my mind was whizzing somewhere between a distant past and the possibilities of the future. Suddenly, I felt like that little girl again, feet thumping, heart racing, blasting through the front door, and stopping suddenly as I saw my mother's face, bright, smiling, *normal.* Back.

I could see that on his face too. He was smiling for real, a smile that actually reached his eyes. Whether it was due to time finally having done its healing or some revelation of sorts, I couldn't say.

"I sure hope it all works out," Daddy replied.

"I hope so too," I added, smiling back as I felt a familiar weight lifting again.

He and Scott continued the conversation with details of how many stalls and this and that and another, regarding that infamous, glorious barn. It looked like that invisible gate had been removed, finally. I couldn't help but wonder about the paths our lives took, and so often they tended to come full circle.

Going back to Fairfield after all these years, wow.

CHAPTER 17

How to Stop a Moving Train 101

Today was a very special day. Not just another beautiful sunny day. It was Daddy's annual battalion reunion. This particular group of WWII veterans have been getting together once a year for several years now. Daddy never misses, if he can help it. They have a bond that can only come from sharing an experience that only they truly understand. The wives as well. They share an understanding uniquely their own. They were the young brides watching helplessly as their husbands were carried away. They, too, stood strong supporting one another.

My thoughts were once again interrupted as Daddy came into the living room dressed to the hilt. He looked so handsome in his brown polyester Western suit, white cotton shirt, and bolo tie with a silver and turquoise medallion. He had on his favorite brown Stetson hat, his dress hat, he called it. His dress cowboy boots were freshly shined and polished.

Mom walked in right behind him. She had her black Western skirt with a white ruffle. Her white blouse with black fringe matched perfectly. She was wearing black cowgirl boots. They looked like they were about to walk right out onto the stage of the Grand Ole Opry.

I couldn't help but smile.

The reunion would be at the Cumberland Mountain State Park. The group reserved the conference room on the lower level of the restaurant. The whole back side of this facility upstairs and down was a wall of windows overlooking the lake. The lake was lined with trees and park benches smartly placed around it. From one side you could see the famous stone bridge dam that has caught the eye of many a painter and photographer. The architecture is very unique with seven stone arches made from our local crab orchard stone that this area is well-known for. It was constructed in the 1930s, the same time as the Homestead project began. I always love coming here for the view as well as the homestyle-cooked food. I was very excited to meet some of Momma and Daddy's old friends from a time that I am sure shaped their lives in ways I will never fully understand.

We loaded up in Momma and Daddy's van and headed north up Lantana road toward Pigeon Ridge road. There we would take a right onto Pigeon Ridge, which would lead us directly into the park. The drive itself was breathtaking. Rolling hills and fields and ponds lined both sides of the curvy road, offset by mountain ridges in the background. This area was appropriately called the Homesteads community. During the Depression, President Roosevelt started the Homestead project here and other rural areas across the country. The community came together and helped build homes for poorer families that would be granted the land to farm. A little like the TV show *Extreme Home Makeover*, I mused. All the homes were made from crab orchard stone, indigenous to the area. The floors, walls, and ceilings were all made by hand-cut solid cedar. They are quite a treasure to own now. Many have been added on to or renovated, and since they were so well-built, most still stand.

Upon arrival, we were instantly greeted at the front door by several older men and women. They were all smiling and shaking hands or hugging one another enthusiastically. Mom, of course, already knew everybody, so she was immediately swept into conversation with a group of ladies. This was my first visit. Therefore, Daddy began to introduce me as his baby daughter Sonda. Folks would probably wonder why my parents were not on the same page as to what my name is, because Momma introduces me as Suni. I just smile and roll with it. Should anyone ask for an explanation, I would try and come up with one.

Suddenly, a fellow walked up. "Marshall, do you remember that train you stopped?" he said excitedly.

I noticed several jeers and smiles as, obviously, they all do remember this train incident.

"You about scared me to death! I just knew it was going to be loaded down with German soldiers!"

I looked at Daddy curiously as he said, "I had forgot all about that."

It was obvious he was the only one that had forgotten.

Another fellow walked up and stuck his hand out toward me. "So you are one of Marshall and Ruby's girls, are ya'?" he asked. I reached forward and shook his hand while answering, "Yes, I'm Suni."

I saw Mom greeting one of the wives with a hug on the other side of the room.

"I'm Roscoe," he said in a deep, gravelly voice.

I knew my eyes light up a bit, I had heard about this one. "It's so nice to meet you!" I said. Almost instantly, the conversation going on beside us caught both our attention. We quickly turned to face the circle of gentlemen to my right.

Roscoe interrupted them, saying, "Well, I remember it!" emphatically.

Then he went on, "Marshall stopped all of a sudden, dead still. You remember how it was then, it was like we were all in tune with each other. When one stopped movin', everybody did. We stood there for a minute or two, and I couldn't hear a thing. I looked around, and no one else did either. I asked Marshall what was going on. He just said a train was comin'. My stomach jerked into a thousand knots, all at once hopin' he was wrong, but knowin' him, he wasn't. I asked him if he was sure, 'cause at that point I still didn't hear anything. He shook his head and said without a doubt there would be train comin' around that bend in just a few minutes and we had better take cover."

Roscoe shook his head and looked at the other fellows standin' around. They nodded their heads and seemed to remember the incident as he was describing it.

"I tried to talk him out of stopping it. If it was full of German soldiers, they would most likely have us outnumbered. We would have been in a lot of trouble."

He turned to look Daddy in the face. "Marshall, do you remember me saying, 'Let's just lay low and let it go on by?'"

Daddy nodded his head, obviously recalling the moment well.

"Remember what you said, Marshall?" he asked directly.

Daddy said, "Yeah, I remember. I figured it was our job to stop it. That's what we was sent over there to do."

Daddy hung his head a bit. "If it had been filled with German soldiers, we needed to stop 'em from doin' whatever they planned down the road, I reckoned."

"Right," Roscoe replied. Then he picked back up with, "Anyway, so we set ourselves up to be facing it head-on as it turned that bend. We waited for several minutes before we could all hear it. Then there it was, just as Marshall had said. I still feel that dreaded rumble as it pulled toward us. With every *chugga chugga*, my heart skipped a beat. We all knew he was right, though, we came all that way to win that war, not just try and survive it. So whatever was on that train, it was our duty to stop it, if we could."

I looked around to see all heads nod in agreement. The he continued telling the story, "Marshall was a heck of a shot. He aimed right for the engine and hit it just right so that train came to a screechin' halt. We were holdin' our breath, preparing for the worst. The doors opened. We aimed and had our fingers placed and ready to fire. First out was the conductor and crew. Then we saw a woman in what appeared to be a nurse's uniform step out, then another and another. Slowly, one by one, they all stepped off the train and lined up, hands in the air. We laid low and still as statues, barely breathin', watchin' every move…real close." He said real low, like he might still be afraid of making a noise.

He took a deep breath and continued, "We waited to make sure no one else was onboard. Then a couple of men in to check."

He wrinkled his forward as if trying to recall the details.

An elderly gentleman shook his head and answered, "Yeah, it was me and Randall. We went in to make sure it was all clear. Randall was killed in battle just a few days later." He explained with an expression that told me Randall had been very important to him.

"Right, I do remember now," Roscoe replied as a look of recollection crossed his brow.

"As it turned out, we'd stopped a train full of German nurses. We had ourselves a field full of cryin' women."

This brought smiles to all the faces in the circle.

"That was a relief!" another gentleman added.

I saw a smile on Daddy's face as he said, "I felt bad about scarin' 'em."

"I went up to the ladies lined up, and they were mumbling in German, of course. I had no idea what they were sayin', so I just tried to tell them we didn't mean no harm to 'em," Daddy explained with a little chuckle.

I heard Roscoe laugh a little as he said, "Yeah, I remember the look on their faces when you were talking to them. They had no idea what you were sayin' either, but I could see them calm right down and start fluttering eyelashes."

Laughter filled the air. Daddy just grinned slyly.

I overheard a lot of reminiscing that day. Every veteran in the room made a point to shake Daddy's hand. I heard many say they would never have made it home if he had not shot that German plane down. They recalled other memories Daddy had already shared with me. They talked about Schnapps, the little boy. I watched as I was filled with such pride to be able to call this man Daddy. I had always known he was my hero. Until now, I had no idea he was also a hero to so many others.

I then decided to go over and meet the ladies Mom was talking with. As I approached, she wrapped her arm around me and began introducing me to the ladies. I smiled and shook their hands. They were reminding one another of this, that, and another, when one lady said, "I just remember Ruby laying on her stomach in the floor and writing Marshall a letter every night before she went to bed." She turned to look at me and smiled. "Back then me and your Mom lived very close together and found a lot of comfort in each other's company. Either I stayed at her house or she stayed at mine almost every night. Then when the war ended and our fellows came back, me and

Ed moved to Ohio. We kind of lost touch after that. But I can tell you we would not have made it without each other then."

I tried to imagine Mom on the floor, legs bent at the knee and ankles crossed, as she wrote her letters. Probably had her long red hair clipped back.

Not for the first time, I sure wished I had those letters and wondered what could have happened to them.

Finally, we all took our places at the banquet tables. We stood as one of the men said a blessing and thanked God wholeheartedly for every day they had been given since the age of eighty. Saying every day afterward was nothing short of a miracle. He thanked God for giving them the gift of their families all coming together that day, expressing a heartfelt gratitude that they had made it back to have families. I marveled at the things we take for granted. He also asked God to bless the souls and families of those that had not been given that gift. There was a moment of silence for remembrance of those less fortunate, such as Randall, I thought.

We sat back down, and I took a quick look around at everyone gathered. Now wrinkled and gray. I tried to imagine them at eighteen, what they would have looked like. I looked at the faces of their children and wives, some with grandchildren. If any of these men had come back broken, you couldn't tell it now. They were smiling and laughing and joking. Sometimes, you might see a small hint of a tear appear as a more difficult memory arose in the conversations.

However, all in all, it appeared they came back with their kindness and, perhaps, hopefulness, even joy, still intact.

I felt a soft nudge and heard Mom say, "What are you smiling about?"

"Oh, I didn't realize I was, actually," I replied.

Then I promptly proceeded to dig in to my meatloaf, mashed potatoes, and rolls. I knew full well that the white cake with peanut butter frosting was sitting on the dessert table waiting just for me.

*****

While writing this book, I always had my Spotify playing in the background. I would put it on my playlist, but inevitably it would go rogue. I am sure that part is normal. Spotify does that. The strange part is that it would play music I had never heard before by artist I was completely unfamiliar with, and every time, the music would go right along with whatever I was writing at that moment. For instance, while writing this part, a song by Christy Nockels started playing and completely caught my attention. In her beautiful voice I heard, "Kissing Momma's cheek and holding Daddy's hand, thank you, Lord, how could I ask for more."

I wondered how she knew.

CHAPTER 18

Marshall Gives Ruby Her Stage, 1994

I heard the crunch of gravel under my tires. It was that familiar sound of coming home. Technically, Fairfield Stables was not where we grew up, as I've explained. But that was where our family could be found those days. You know what they say, home is where the heart is. Now don't get me wrong. I do believe old homeplaces and structures we grow up in or spend lots of time in throughout our lives are special. However, they are only special because of the memories and love they hold. I swear, whether they are good or bad, the energy we create seeps through each and every wall, nail, and thread, and it is easy to feel upon entering.

To hear Larry tell it, Mom did not want to have anything to do with those stables. Daddy tried to coax her into coming to work the office. She flat refused. Said she did not want to work around horses. This conversation went back and forth until, well, did I mention Daddy was stubborn? He had a way of convincing people to do things and have them doing them before they realized they had changed their minds. Perhaps I have mentioned that as well. Talking Mom into working at a stable with big, scary horses certainly tested his skills. He promised her she would never have to go near the horses. She could wear her heels and pumps, and there would be no need to change her style.

After all, it was office work.

Surprisingly, many promises and sweet grins later, she agreed. There were rules, though. Rule number 1 was that she would never ever wear Western clothing. Rule number 2 was she would not go near the animals. Ever. Never. At all. To either of the above.

Right.

By the time Larry made a return visit, since he was the farrier, he hardly recognized his own mother. For she had traded her pumps of many colors and Jackie O.–style dresses for ruffles and fringe and matching boots and cowgirl hats in every color. Then, much more to our surprise, she donned her first pair of blue jeans. I had never seen my mom in jeans before! If you had said I would one day, I'd have bet my last dollar that would never happen.

Daddy encouraged her to plan events and market the stables to the tourists visiting Fairfield Glade. He wanted to make it a big success instead of the sleepy little riding stables that saw only a few visitors here and there. To that point, the stables barely held its own but had not been a profitable amenity for the resort.

She took that as a challenge. She attended board meetings and fought for the support they needed for improvements and supplies. She presented her ideas to up the attraction. Some of the board members wanted to just close the stables. Others wanted to keep it going. Hiring her and Daddy had been a last-ditch effort to make a go of it. The board, even those reluctant to close it, were still were very hesitant to put the funds into it that it needed. Mom used that oh-so-powerful mom finger more than once when faced with doubt and even ridicule. I do believe they had all met their match. Daddy often went with her to the meetings and snickered as he watched her *not* take no for an answer. She had big plans and was determined to see them through.

In reality, they were probably afraid to say no. I would have been. After all, we called her Ruby Red for a reason. In the end, she received the financial support to buy more horses, supplies, and all that was necessary to make her plan a reality.

Tuesday nights became Western Night, with pony rides for the kids and wagon rides through Dodge City. It did not take her long to have the place buzzing with folks from all fifty states. Soon, they were operating in the black. The guided trails stayed booked to capacity on a daily basis. Tuesday nights had gotten very popular, and my sisters had been telling me I needed to come check it out.

When I pulled in, I noticed a parking lot full of cars from Illinois, Indiana, Michigan, Michigan, Michigan, Ohio, Michigan, Florida, oh, yeah, and Michigan. Wyndham had purchased a modular home for Momma and Daddy to live in so they could stay on-site. After all, taking care of up to thirty horses was a 24-7 job. Especially when the horses got creative and decided to escape their confines. They often acted like teenagers. There was always a party somewhere, right?

As we exited our minivan, I stopped for a second to breath in the beautiful view. The stables sat atop a knoll surrounded by the beautiful Tennessee mountains. From there, I could see Renegade Mountain, Black Mountain, and a few others no one has formerly introduced me to. They were vibrant with fall colors of orange, red, green, and yellow. To my left,

I saw the big, infamous barn with a red metal roof. Directly in front was a large concreted area with a gazebo set up with musical instruments and amps ready for a party. The dance floor was between the stage and the white chairs and tables that had been set up. There was a covered wagon that had lots of food being laid out. I took a deep breath of the clean mountain air and thought, *I don't blame them. I'd come here too from…wherever.*

Then I headed toward all the activity. I saw Daddy leaned over, hands on his knees, eye level to a group of young admirers of his, or Big John's, I wasn't sure. He was holding a set of reigns hooked to the amazon of a horse. We had had him for years, and I felt like I grew up on Big John's back. When I was younger, I would lead him up to the fence and have to climb to the top to get on. I would actually still have to do that. I remember riding him through open fields all over Cumberland Mountain Retreat. He had the smoothest racking gate of any horse I had ever ridden. It felt as if I was on a magic flying carpet.

I was stood close by a little boy holding the hand of an older gentleman. I overheard the little boy say in amazement, "Look! Grandpa. It's a *real* cowboy" while dragging out the *real*. I had to bite my lower lip and hold in a giggle. Yep, and there he was. Daddy was dressed to the hilt: dark denim dress jeans, a denim jacket to match, a white western shirt, a red bandana bolo tie, a white cowboy hat, and his brown dress boots, polished and shined for the occasion. He had on a silver belt buckle that had his name engraved on it with a few turquois stone accents.

Smart kid.

I watched as Daddy explained how a horse had to be taken care of. How to hold the reigns when you rode. Signals you used to let the horse know what you want him or her to do. How you sat straight in the saddle. He explained, "You can't let a horse in the barn with the food where he can just eat all he wants. They will founder," I heard him say. "What's founder?" said one little fellow. Then Daddy explained, "It's a real serious bellyache." Another little boy said with wide eyes, "Oh, I did that once." The other kids acknowledged they had foundered a time or two as well. Then one little girl asked, "Why do you put those metal shoes on them? Does it hurt?" Daddy said, "Well, that's a good question for my son, Larry. He is the farrier…that is, he puts the shoes on them and trims the hooves. Unfortunately, he ain't here right now, so I'll try and answer it best I can." He took a breath and said, "They have to have those shoes to protect their feet, just like yours do. They can't really feel anything when you put them on. It's like your fingernails or your hair. It don't hurt when you cut your hair, right?" Daddy asked the group. They all shook their heads and agreed, cutting your hair didn't hurt. "Right," he said, "so you have to trim the hooves just like your hair or fingernails, and then you can put the horses' shoes on them and their feet won't hurt." In unison, they said, "Ohhhhhh." There were lots of questions from his little crowd, and then he took them one by one and led them on a short ride around a circle.

He was certainly in his element.

I looked over and Mom too was enjoying herself as the belle of the ball. She had on her white boots and matching hat and a turquoise skirt with a ruffled hem. Her shirt was turquoise with white piping around the collar and cuffs with contrasting fringe. What kind of Western outfit would be complete without fringe? She was talking to people, welcoming guests, directing food setup, and honestly, having a blast.

I heard an announcement that it was time to load the wagon for another round. One group of guests was exiting and another would load. Mom looked over and saw me and the kids and waved us toward the wagon and let me know we were to get onboard. I love hayrides and hadn't been on one since the last family reunion about a year before, so I was more than happy to do what I was told. We headed over obediently. I saw Daddy hand the reins of Big John to the fellow who had just exited the driver's seat of the wagon and who then took over the rides with the kids. Oh good, Daddy was going to drive the wagon.

He walked over, climbed up, and took the driver's seat. I heard him say, "Everybody ready?" The crowd roared an emphatic "Yes!" I heard his familiar

"Hiyaaa" as he barely moved the reigns he was holding. Away we went as the team of Belgians, Barney and Cindy, that is, started leading us out toward the open field. Barney and Cindy were obviously stars of this show and had their own fans. They knew the routine by heart and hardly needed prodding. We turned toward the wooded area that was approximately five hundred yards or so across the field behind the barn.

We only got about halfway across the field when we saw bandits running over the hill to our right. They had bandanas disguising their faces, but I knew who at least four of them were—Connie, Carolina, Tim, and Larry. I saw they had rounded up accomplices as well. They stopped the wagon, and one of them, holding a stick, straight up, said, "This is a stickup." Everybody laughed. It turned out no one had anything worth taking. One little boy offered his prechewed bubblegum and the wrapper. An adorable little girl with curly blond hair offered her half-eaten sucker. She looked to be about four and reminded me of Shirley Temple.

There were a few more *Hee Haw*–type shenanigans, and we were on our way to the wooded area. As we rounded the bend, we entered Dodge City, indicated by a large, carved entrance sign that hung between two trees. To the left was a saloon with girls decked out in their costumes, gamblers, and cowboys. Suddenly there was a shoot-out and a damsel in distress, and the sheriff had to haul a bank robber to the jailhouse where the moonshiner was already locked up. Wow, we barely made it out alive. When we got through Dodge City, we came back out into the clearing on the other side of the field. Suddenly, we heard more hollerin' and whoopin', and it seemed we might be getting attacked by Indians. On the other side came the cowboys, and they chased one another around a few fast and exciting circles, showing off a bit of skill, which everyone in my family seemed to inherit but me, and then off they went, back into the woods behind us.

It was all very exciting, and I worked up an appetite. It was time to fill our plates with roasted hot dogs, baked beans, potato salad, and chips. While everyone was eating, the sun began to set with such brilliant colors it rivaled the trees. There was a string of twinkling lights beginning to show around the eating and dancing area, and I heard music begin to play.

Mom took the stage with her band and began playing guitar and singing and yodeling. She sang and played and yodeled some more, always, always, smiling ear to ear. Everyone seemed to love it. People got up and two-stepped and fast-stepped and twirled and do-si-doed until the stars shone brightly overhead.

"So all this happens *every* Tuesday night?" I asked Connie and Carolina.

They smiled and said, "Yep."

I decided to come back more often on Tuesday, perhaps the next time joining the bandits.

I watched them, Momma on her stage, literally playing her dreams, and Daddy right there in the midst of it all. I realized, you actually *can* have your cake and eat it too. I'd heard Momma say many times, "What's the point in having a cake if you can't eat it!" Then I recalled a few more momisms such as, "We ought to be thankful to Adam and Eve. If it weren't for them, we wouldn't have all these pretty clothes to wear!" There were many more, but I think that one was my personal favorite. She was definitely more of a glass-half-full-type person.

Momma and Daddy managed to have all us kids (how lucky can you get, really?) in spite of the naysaying doctors and horrific obstacles they both had to deal with. Then here we were, watching her perform in front of a very appreciative audience, thanks to Daddy.

To the very end, when any doctor put a stethoscope up to Momma's heart, the reaction was shock and awe. They would get wide-eyed and jerk back and ask, "How are you alive?!" Many times, surgery had been offered and suggested, but Mom always said that she was better off not risking it and opted to let it go as long as God allowed. She passed away at the age of ninety-one.

They both ended up running the Dorchester Riding Stables in Fairfield for fourteen years. When Daddy became unable to do so, Mom then had to be a full-time caregiver for him and Granny, so they both retired in 1999. They returned once again to the Winesap end of Cumberland County. Daddy often recalled the days at the Dorchester Stables, wistfully saying, "Those were good times."

They made lots of friends there that would often come to visit them at the old homeplace, long after they retired. They also had some rather different experiences at those stables, such as one time a little private plane was having engine trouble and emergency landed in the field with a thump. Daddy watched it coming down from the front porch and bounce abruptly to a stop. He just said, "Well, that's different." Then he went out to see what he could do to help. The pilot got out, scratching his head and eyeing his failed aircraft. He was unharmed, but his plane, after an examination, was found to be in need of a part he would have to locate and repair before he could take off again. He ended up staying with Momma and Daddy a few days. I found a letter he wrote to them later. It stated that, as it turned out, that was one of the best days of his life, oddly enough. He said getting to know them was truly a blessing and made it all worth it. He then thanked them wholeheartedly for their hospitality and kindness, saying it was something he would never forget.

That's Momma and Daddy all right. They always had that effect on people. They loved every minute they spent at that stables, meeting so many wonderful people over the years.

The last family reunion Daddy was able to attend, he asked Uncles Paul, James, and Raymond to take him back out to the stables in Fairfield. He had not been able to drive for some time, and he had not been out there for a year or more. They were happy to oblige. While Momma and Daddy ran the stables, we had had many reunions and gatherings there as well as weddings and celebrations. Everyone had fond memories of those days. What happened once Dad and his brothers arrived left them all shocked and awed.

As they pulled up to the barn, they saw the horses way off out into the field. Daddy, being short of breath and unable to move quickly, made his way to the fence railing. His brothers following alongside. Once again, as he so often did, he stepped one foot on the first rail and crossed his arms on the top. He looked out across the field then lifted his white Stetson hat into the air and gave it a circular motion as he whistled. It was obviously an inviting and familiar sound to the grazing animals. For they all stopped, raised their heads, and looked up intently. Then started walking briskly toward the fence. One by one, they lined up and took turns nuzzling him sweetly, even reverently. One by one. Uncle Paul said he had never seen anything like it.

See, I told you they knew.

Daddy was correct in saying those days at the stables were *good times*.

Yes, they sure were.

CHAPTER 19

Daddy and Christine's Dream

I crept quietly into the house. I had arrived early and didn't want to wake anyone. I was not surprised to find Mom already in the kitchen.

"Good morning," I said quietly while kissing her cheek.

"Good morning," she said with a smile.

"Everybody sleep okay last night?" I asked.

She got a bit of a worried frown in her brow. "Well, your dad is not sleeping well. He was up and down all night." She took a deep breath, dropping her shoulders. "He does that a lot," she explained.

The sad expression in her eyes mirrored my own. I reminded myself to be thankful, thankful he had made it home from that awful war, thankful he lived through starvation and hepatitis, not to mention all the other obstacles I was thankful he survived. Fifty, thirty, even twenty years ago, if God himself had said, "Don't worry. He will live until he is eighty-two, and he will raise six kids and see nineteen grandkids burst into life," I would have thought that would be enough. That day, it just didn't seem so. I tried to imagine life without him, not having that calm voice to still my often-fearful soul. When I needed his words of wisdom, where would I go? Where would we all go? Just be thankful, I reminded myself, again. I had today. Today was good.

She didn't stop moving, stirring, cooking, and always making sure to have breakfast ready for her patients' arising. Daddy was so weak in those days. It was a big deal to make it out to sit on the front porch. Granny was pretty much bedridden. Being the primary caretaker was taking its toll on Mom. We all helped, of course. However, it was more than just the tasks of caretaking. It was the heartbreaking and slow release of the two people that had walked with her throughout her whole life, the parts that no one else could ever relate to or understand. She and Daddy were coming up on their sixtieth wedding anniversary.

Granny always had to have her oatmeal and reiterated every morning how you had to eat your oats. I couldn't argue. She would see her 101st birthday that year.

As that thought was processing, Mom asked, "Want breakfast?" I looked at her and said, "Yeah, I'll have whatever Granny is havin'." She smiled, knowing full well what was running through my mind. Granny's body, per se, was still in pretty good shape. I recalled seeing her lying on her side with the blanket wrapped around her midsection. Her legs were sticking out uncovered, slightly bent. I couldn't help but notice how smooth her skin was. How perfectly her legs were shaped thighs down. She could almost pass for a teenager. Mom had said my sisters and I got our great legs from Granny, just like she had. I smiled to myself, thankful for that too.

"Here," I said to her softly, "I'll take Granny her breakfast." I took the steaming-hot bowl of oatmeal and put a little honey and butter on top. I went to the drawer where our utensils were kept for 40 years, 50? And picked up a teaspoon. Knowing the routine, I poured a glass of milk and set it all on a serving tray.

I turned toward the hallway leading to the bedrooms. As I walked past the first one, I saw Daddy through the slightly opened door. He was beginning to stir. I stopped for just a second and watched as he slowly made his way to an upright position. He carefully laid his feet on the floor. His head was bent down as if willing his feet to have the strength to hold him upright. They were getting less and less trust-worthy for their job.

I could see his face clearly. He was looking at the picture on his nightstand beside the bed. I couldn't see the picture, but I had a million times. I knew it by heart. It was Mom. She sat at a sewing machine. She worked for a manufacturing company called the Pikeville Shirt Factory. She had told us her boss wanted them to come in ready to have their pictures taken, and she did. She wore a white sleeveless V-neck dress. You cannot see this part in the picture, but I knew her dress was seemed to a perfect fit and showing the hourglass shape of her slim figure. She had on a string of pearls with matching earrings. Most evident was her big smile full of bright-white teeth. Atop her head was a perfectly constructed pile of red hair sprayed enough to withstand the winds of a hurricane. Last but not least, bright-red lipstick. There was a time when Mom would not be seen without her bright-red lipstick. Also, not evident in the picture, but I could see it plain as day, would be the hose and closed-toed pumps. I remember as a young child looking at the wall of shelves filled with boxes of pumps in every color. I wondered briefly what had happened to all those beautiful high-heeled shoes.

Then I saw it, that *look*. It wasn't the first time. That soulful, forlorn, heartbreaking expression. It often appeared when he didn't know anyone was looking. He would look at her as if she was still just slightly out of reach. We were all aware of Mom's dreams. How she had been offered an opportunity to go after them. I had heard the slight hint of loss in her voice a time or two.

Watching closely, I could feel more than see that he was still wondering if he had somehow thwarted those dreams, wondering if he had been *enough*. Perhaps he thought he failed on some level to make her truly happy. He had never told her she couldn't go after them. I had never seen him try and stop her from doing anything she wanted to do. However, life has a funny way of taking the best-made plans and doing something else entirely.

Communication was not always their strongest point. I knew that had been a bone of contention for Mom, especially. She longed to hear flowery words of love and see romantic gestures. Those kinds of things did not come natural to him. As I watched, I thought of how hard he had worked all his life. Then how unfair life had been to him. Just when he was about to really succeed, tragedy stuck. Then how he and Mom stood strongly together and made sure we all made it through.

He was the calm, the hope we all held onto in times of trouble like that lifeboat that saved him once. Again, I saw those waves that tried to wash him away and felt a slight shudder. Those waves were getting close again.

I remember getting upset that life just was not going the way I intended it to. I'd hear his words, "Aw, Sonda [at least now I know where that name came from], don't take everything to heart. It will all work itself out in the end." He was right, always. I wondered for a second what on earth we would do without being able to hear his voice guiding, grounding us. The very sound alone made the world a safer place. That sly grin was what kept it turning, I'm pretty sure.

I trembled slightly and caused the glass to clink against the bowl on my tray. I took a deep breath as I tried to steady the tray as well as myself. His head jerked up and caught me looking at him. He saw the welling in my eyes. He had it too. Instantly he knew he had shared, inadvertently, a small piece of his burdened soul.

Then I pictured Mom. I saw her smiling, *happy,* playing her guitar. We were her audience, at least prior to performing in Fairfield. Then I remember how excited she and Daddy got with each new grandchild. Everyone as exciting as the first. Momma didn't just want a stage, she wanted this too. Him too. I couldn't help but wonder, *How can he not know how very much he has been to her, to us?*

It occurred to me suddenly I had been a bit like a Peeping Tom caught in the act. I smiled at him warmly with all the love in my heart and continued toward Granny's room. My hands were still a bit shaky, but I tried to sit carefully on her bedside and compose myself lest we have hot oatmeal in our laps.

"Hey, Granny," I said, but it came out more like a squeak. She faced me, and I asked her if she was ready for breakfast.

I heard Connie's voice as she came through the front door. She was saying her good-mornings. I was relieved to hear her voice, knowing she was there to help get Granny ready to go to her doctor's appointment. Sometimes it actually took a village. Mom had laid out a pair of blue polyester pull-on pants with an elastic waist to make dressing her easy. The shirt she had out to go with it was white with little blue flowers that matched. When Connie came back to Granny's room and said "Hello," I returned her smile. Then I went back to helping Granny. Suddenly Connie said, "Do you think Daddy is okay? He seems a little distraught." I thought about what I had seen earlier, and my heart stumbled a bit. I had heard her and Daddy talking, but they were too far away for me to understand what they were saying.

I turned toward her and asked, "What did he say?"

She thought for a second. "He says he needs to go see Christine." She looked at me with concern lining her face and continued, "Right away." Neither of us were sure what to make of his sudden hurry to see Aunt Christine.

Then we quieted to listen as we heard Daddy say, "Ruby, do you think we can go see Christine today or tomorrow?"

Momma replied, "I'd love to do that, but I have to take Granny in to town today for her checkup, and the house is a mess. I have so much laundry to do. Plus, we'll need to get someone to sit with Granny. The ride would be too hard for her. Let me work it out, and we'll go this weekend."

We heard him say, "Okay, that should be okay." There was worry and maybe something else in his voice. We gave each other a concerned look.

Our attention was jerked quickly back to the task at hand as Granny exclaimed while she pointed at the pretty little white-with-blue-flowers blouse, "I am *not* wearin' that ugly thing! I want *my* shirt!" We had already successfully gotten the pants on her. They were a royal blue.

Connie said simply, "Uh-oh." Sometimes Granny and Mom went rounds over what Granny wore. Mom would say Granny embarrassed her to death, insisting on wearing her shirt. We would laugh and call Granny Charlie Brown. Sure enough, we had dozens of pictures going back thirty years showing Granny in that same blouse. It had certainly seen better days. It was a really ugly polyester/cotton blend, stretchy, stained, faded, holey red-and-green shirt with three missing buttons on the collar. Mom had tried to throw it away many times. But after all, Granny is one hundred.

Finally, we had Granny ready to go see her doctor in, yes, her favorite, ugly, worn-out shirt. Mom was not happy. We, the village, helped her into the van and strapped her in safely. With a sigh of relief, I watched as Connie and Mom pulled out of the circle drive to head toward town.

Connie was assigned to help Momma with Granny that day. My job was to sit with Daddy. *I am the lucky one*, I thought to myself. I needed see if I could find out what had him so determined to get to Aunt Chris all of a sudden.

I bounced back into the house, and by then, Daddy was sitting in his chair. He had on his light cotton pajamas and a light-gray cotton housecoat. He couldn't stand to wear material that had any weight to it at all, only a very, very thin, barely-there substance. His skin was as thin as the material and tightly wrapped around his fragile bones. At that point, he weighed about 115 pounds. He rarely left the house and didn't like to be alone. We made sure someone was with him at all times. We were very protective of our turn to stay with him. He told us his stories. Sometimes they were about Grandma and Grandpa or things he and Mom did. War stories, of course. And we ate Little Debbie cakes.

I was anxious to see what was on his mind. "Need another cup of coffee?" I asked him as I came back in the door. "Sure," he said. I went into the kitchen and began to pour us both one, each with cream. I was a little anxious. I wasn't sure why, though. It seemed there was something weighing heavily on his mind.

I walked back in and set his cup beside him. He was sitting in his recliner. His recliner was pretty spiffy. It lifted and swirled and swung and did all kinds of things when the kids were in it. That day, it was still. He, too, sat motionless. Then he slowly reached for his coffee and took a small sip. I could tell he was trying to form words or a thought. I looked him in the eye and asked, "What's wrong, Daddy?"

"I had the strangest dream last night," he began.

"Oh, really?" I took a breath and asked, "What was it?"

He looked at me and explained. "It was about Christine. It was like one of those dreams my mom used to tell us about when we were kids. She knew to trust her instincts and had better ones than most."

I sipped my coffee and hoped he might take a sip, too, to stave away a chill I knew we both felt, not that it was cold. It was a beautiful spring day, in fact. After a few moments, he continued, "This dream… it's not letting me go. I *need* to see Christine," he said firmly. "Try as I might, I can't get it off my mind."

That's when he told me about the white book. He had dreamed that he and Christine were fighting over a white book. Chris ran off and hid it from him. She wouldn't let him have it back and kept telling him, "Me first."

"Did you guys have a special white book when you were kids?" I asked.

"No," he replied.

224

I could tell he was visibly shaken. "What does that mean?" I asked.

"I don't know," he said, shaking his head.

We turned our attention to *TV Land*. I had hoped to take his mind off the dream for a bit. We would go see Aunt Chris that Saturday in just a few more days.

While the guns of *Gunsmoke* were blasting and Festus was handing out his quotes of wisdom, I struggled to understand what I had seen earlier. That look on Daddy's face when I had inadvertently spied on him through the crack in the door and that haunting sadness I couldn't quite place, was there some connection to Aunt Chris and Mom stirring that I didn't understand? I looked over at him and knew instantly that redirecting his attention to *Gunsmoke* was not helping him any more than it was me. "Daddy?" I said. "Want a Little Debbie?"

"That'd be good," he said, slightly shaking his head. I jumped up to go grab a few. I started to take one out so we could split it but stopped. No, I took two. Then I stopped myself again. Finally, I just grabbed the whole box. With the other hand, I grabbed two glasses and the half-gallon of milk out of the fridge and headed back in. I thought we might need supplies.

I sat down, poured us each a glass of milk, and started opening packages. I was trying to think of a way to broach the subject. After all, I had stumbled, uninvited, into a very private part of him, and I knew it. How could I ask something when I couldn't figure out what the question should be?

"You know Christine…" he said, getting my attention quickly. "She was a little leery of your mom at first." My eyes popped wide with surprise. Yes, that was the question I couldn't put my finger on. Mom had said something along those lines before. So perhaps there was some connection to that dream, to Mom, and to that *forlorn* expression. "At first, ya see, Ruby, well, she wanted so bad to be a singer. Go on the Grand Ole Opry and be like Patsy Cline. She could've done it too. She's got the talent. She actually was on the *Cas Walker Show* once. That was before you were born."

I nodded that I had actually heard about that.

He chuckled, recalling, "Connie was the baby then. She was only three or four maybe. I'll never forget when she saw her momma on the TV, it scared her. She ran up and was kissing it and saying, 'Momma, get out of there!' Then she ran around to the back of it and looked over the top." We were both laughing. "She kept tellin' me to get her momma outta there!" Then he went on, "Your momma had the opportunity. She could've had a contract and everything." Then there it was again, that *look*. "I guess I never quite understood why she married me. She had always said she was going to move to the city and be a singer. When she wrote me back sayin' yes to my letter, I was right surprised."

I had never imagined that. How is it we never see that at one time our parents were young and in love, vulnerable, and worried they'll be heartbroken or their feelings will not be reciprocated? I just sat there waiting for the rest of the story.

He took another sip of his milk to wash down the Debbie cake. "Chris was always real protective. She worried Ruby wouldn't be happy." The word did not come out easily. Then I saw the concern in his eyes again. "Chris has always tried to protect me," he reiterated sternly, giving me a very concerned and direct look as we both felt that slight chill in the warm spring air.

Saturday came more slowly than usual. I think we were all anxious. Daddy had told me he had had that dream again, stronger and more vivid than before. It was so unlike him to put weight on such things. He was not a spiritual man, per se. At least not by most folks' standards. It was definitely out of character, and I was not sure what to make of it. He was always very practical, yet there he was, obviously shaken by that dream. It was confusing, to say the least.

I arrived early to go with them to see Aunt Chris. I had hoped after seeing her he would be able to rest easy, which was something he had not been able to do. I had always heard that having a dream multiple times was supposed to mean something, but for the life of me, I couldn't figure out what a dream about a white book could possibly mean. I got the distinct feeling he knew something about it the rest of us did not understand.

Momma and Daddy were still getting ready to leave when we heard a car at a faster than normal speed, pulling up the gravel drive. Mom ran to the window and stopped suddenly. She was peering out at the oncomer. I didn't know who it was, but I could tell by the look on her face something was wrong. She looked at me and said in a fear-laden voice, "It's Hughel and JoAnn." Them coming to see us wasn't that unusual, and certainly they were not always bearers of bad news. We got together often under happy circumstances. *This*, however, was not normal. I could feel it as well as she could before we caught sight of their faces. We opened the door and met them before they made it to the front porch. JoAnn had tears in her eyes and began to explain, "Chris has had a stroke. She is in intensive care in Lenoir City hospital." Lenoir City is where Chris and her husband, Jerry, had made their home for the past several years. It was only an hour away.

Connie saw Aunt JoAnn and Uncle Hughel pull in from her kitchen window. She, too, knew immediately, something was not right. She came running down, and we scurried to get out the door. We decided I would ride with them. Connie would stay with Granny until the sitter arrived, and she would let the others know about the turn of events.

We headed east. As we were driving, JoAnn began to explain that Chris had been acting very odd that past week. Jerry, her husband, had said she got up one morning a few days before and started loading her purse and belongings in her walker. She told Jerry she needed to go see Marshall, *insisted* she had to go see Marshall. Jerry said she kept tryin' to get out the door with or without him. It was all Jerry could do to calm her down. He, too, had promised to bring her to her brother's that Saturday. Jerry said she kept talking about a white book. She had had a dream about her and Marshall fighting over a white book. She said she was determined not to let him have it first. Jerry could not understand what she was talking about.

I felt totally bewildered. What did it mean? What was that white book?

I heard Momma say, "Marshall, you're white as a ghost! Are you okay?" Then I watched him as he obviously struggled to tell them about the dream. He explained to them how he had felt somethin' was wrong and wanted to get to her. I could tell by the look on Momma's face she had regretted not going sooner. Then he said, "Ruby, this is not your fault. You did the best you could."

I turned my head to look out of the window, trying to keep my tears quiet and hidden. I wondered in awe about the bond we have with our siblings. *Do we all have this?* I wondered. I concluded, *I hope so.*

The rest of the ride was very quiet. I think we were struggling to understand what all of it could possibly mean. We arrived at the hospital in record time. Uncle Hughel pulled up to the covered area to drop everyone off at the door. I jumped out and ran to the other side, opening the door for Daddy and Mom. We made our way inside and immediately saw the rest of the family. Aunt Margie, Bill, Paul, and Rosemary, Paul's wife, were already there as well as several of the kids—the cousins is how we referred to each other. I lost count a long time before as to how many cousins I had. I guess we wanted to make sure the world had enough Tabors. There was no chance of running out.

It would have looked like a family reunion if the surroundings were not so cold and sterile. I realized it was amazing what those familiar faces did for us when our hearts were sinking. We all started chatting, talking about what the doctors were saying, how Christine seemed to be. From all I heard, she was not responding. We had to take turns going back to see her. Only a few at a time were allowed in ICU. Everyone was waiting anxiously for one of the family members to come out so the next one could go in.

I noticed Daddy was quickly losing his breath and needed to sit down as soon as possible. Momma had fussed at him for years to try and get him to quit smoking. I would've given anything if he would have listened. I looked around frantically to find a place for him to sit when my cousin Mike, my aunt Helen's son, appeared from nowhere with a wheelchair in hand. He always tried to look out for everybody, being the good fellow he was. I smiled and said, "Thank you." We got Daddy seated and comfortable. I turned to give Mike a hug since I had not seen him since the last family reunion. By then the whole room was filled with new arrivals constantly coming in. I could see the hospital receptionist's eyes open wide. She probably wondered how many family members one woman could have. Little did she know, those who lived faraway were in the process of catching flights or loading up their vehicles and heading there as quickly as they could as well. Some of my cousins were busy arranging rooms in the hotel next to the hospital for those staying the night.

One thing my family did was stick tight and take care of one another. I felt the familiar comfort I had years ago while sleeping in a sleeping bag alongside all of them on our living room floor.

All heads turned at the sound of big double doors swinging open. Looking up, we saw Jerry and Geraldine, Aunt Chris's husband and daughter, walking out. They were looking pretty grim. As everyone gathered together, I heard JoAnn telling Polly and Paul about the dream. Jerry and Geraldine were listening and looked at one another with wide-eyed wonder. So many more questions than answers.

A voice said, "Who would like to go in next?" It was the nurse at the station. Polly quickly replied, "Me and Marshall want to go in next. At that, I jumped up and grabbed Daddy's wheelchair handles and started rolling him toward the door. I was afraid to ask permission to go in with them, so I tried to look needed.

I rolled him down the corridor behind Aunt Polly. When we got to Chris's room, Polly held open the door for me to push Daddy in. I stalled at the sight of poor Aunt Chris. She looked so frail and lifeless. Gone was the bright, sophisticated-looking, beautiful lady I had always known. I remembered the Aunt Christine that took me to see *Disney on Ice* when I was young. It was the most amazing thing I had ever seen. It was my first experience with a live performance of that kind, and I was *awed*.

Daddy interrupted my thoughts when he said weakly, "Put me up close to her." I didn't say anything, just rolled him up to her bedside as closely as I could get. Polly stepped around to the other side of Chris's bed. I saw Daddy reach out and take hold of Christine's hand. Instantly, her eyes popped open. I jumped a little, surprised. She had not been responsive, at least according to what I had heard out in the lobby.

"Christine," Daddy said, leaning close to her, smiling his bravest smile. "I want my book back."

Christine's eyes welled up, and she pulled on Daddy's hand, trying hard to raise her head and speak. Her mouth was moving oddly, and she made a few noises, trying to get the words out, struggling, gripping tightly. Then we heard it. She said, drawing her words out in a breathless sound, "Me first, Marshall." She caught a bit of air again and strained out, "I'll see you there." Daddy had big tears rolling down his cheeks to match hers. Polly and I looked at each other, mouths open, a look of wonder and shock on our faces.

That night, I pushed Daddy up close to the window of his hotel room. It was directly across from Christine's room. She, too, had been rolled up closely in front of the window, her bed raised to be able to see her brother across a narrow-paved drive. They could see each other clearly. I watched as she lifted her frail hand and waved weakly at Daddy across the short distance. He did the same.

Shortly after, she was gone. Determined to go first.

I asked Aunt Polly later what she thought the white book was. She said it was the Book of Life. I have no other explanation.

Daddy and his siblings shared a bond unlike any I have ever seen. A few months before Daddy passed away, Aunt JoAnn and Uncle Hughel brought Hershel to see him. Both were in very bad health. Hershel was in a wheelchair and had Parkinson's disease. Unable to speak, his wheelchair was rolled up beside Daddy. We had put a hospital bed in the living room so he would not be separated from everyone. He was raised slightly, looking anxiously at his brother. Hershel reached out and held Daddy's hand tightly. His eyes were filled with tears, and though he could not mouth the words, "I love you" poured from his very soul. The air itself seemed to be whispering goodbye.

As it would happen, Christine passed away on July 25, 2006, after beating Daddy in the race to go first. Then Daddy went to join her December 23, 2006. He waited twenty minutes past his and Mom's sixty-third wedding anniversary date. It meant a lot to Mom that he hung in there and didn't leave on the date in which they married. She was so nervous all day of the twenty-second, and I believe Daddy knew it even though he was not able to say so. Thankfully, they were able to say their goodbyes. I peered from the kitchen into the living room as they were sitting side by side on the edge of his bed. Her head laid on his shoulder and his leaned on hers. They had their arms wrapped tightly around each other just as they had in the picture taken the day he left for service. I stood quietly, listening, whether I should have or not, as I heard his weak and weary voice say "Momma," as he referred to her then, "I love you and the kids so much, but I am so tired."

"I know," she replied. "It's okay. We will be okay."

It seemed to be enough to give him permission to let go of that rope for good.

Only a few days later Aunt JoAnn and all the rest of us sat around him on the floor, the couch, and chairs as we pulled out tons of old pictures and reminisced of days gone by. It actually was a joyous occasion. We felt joy to have been a part of and witness to such a beautiful life.

That house, our home, has always been so full. So very, very *full*.

ABOUT THE AUTHOR

Suni Nelson resides in Crossville Tennessee with her huge and amazing family. Her 'day' job is selling real estate in the retirement community of Fairfield Glade. In between selling real estate she decided to attend writing school and fulfil a lifelong dream of becoming a writer. Her greatest honor was to be handed these very true and personal stories from her parents.